THE CHRISTIAN SOCIAL HISTORY SERIES

How OUR NATION BEGAN

DON SHARKEY

SISTER MARGARET
S.H., S.N.D. de N.

**Rt. Rev. Msgr.
PHILIP J. FURLONG**

• • •

Technical Editors
Walter L. Willigan, Ph. D.
John Reddington, M. A.

Artists
John C. Wonsetler
H. B. Vestal • J. Lewis Pellicer
Don Lambo • Alex Sniffen
Frank Schwarz • Christie McFall

How Our Nation Began

Don Sharkey.
Sister Margaret, S.H., S.N.D. de N.
Rt. Rev. Msgr Philip J. Furlong

Technical Editors
Walter L. Willigan, Ph.D.
John Reddington, M.A.

Artists:
John C. Wonsetler, H.B. Vestal,
J. Lewis Pellicer, Don Lambo
Alex Sniffen, Frank Schwarz, and Christie McFall

Hillside Education

Copyright © 2017, Hillside Education

Originally published in 1954 by W.H. Sadlier, Inc.

Nihil Obstat:

JOHN M. A. FEARNS, S.T.D.

Imprimatur:

✠ FRANCES CARDINAL SPELLMAN
Archbishop of New York
August 15, 1854

Cover image: *Betsy Ross 1777* by Jean Leon Gerome Ferris, courtesy of Wikimedia

Cover design by Mary Jo Loboda

All rights reserved. No part of this publication may be reproduced in whole or in part, stored in a retrieval system or transmitted in any form or by any means, electronic, mechanical, photocopying, recording, or otherwise, without prior written permission of the publisher.

ISBN: 978-0-9976647-9-9

Hillside Education
475 Bidwell Hill Road
Lake Ariel, PA 18436
www.hillsideeducation.com

CONTENTS

UNIT ONE: How America Was Discovered 4
   1. The Indians Were the First Americans 8
   2. The Northmen Find America 14
   3. The Holy Wars 20
   4. Marco Polo Visits the Far East 28
   5. Prince Henry's Sailors 32
   6. Christopher Columbus 38
   7. People in Europe Learn about America 48

UNIT TWO: New Homes in the New World 56
   8. The Spaniards Settle in the South 58
   9. The English Settle at Jamestown 68
  10. The French Settle in the North 76
  11. The Dutch Settle in New York 90

UNIT THREE: Thirteen Growing Colonies 100
  12. Pilgrims and Puritans Come to New England 102
  13. People Come to the Middle Colonies 114
  14. The Southern Colonies 124
  15. How People Lived in the English Colonies 130

UNIT FOUR: A New Nation 144
  16. The French Lose Their Land in North America 146
  17. The Colonists Declare Their Freedom 156
  18. Americans Win Their Freedom 168

Unit One
HOW AMERICA WAS DISCOVERED

LOOKING INTO THE LONG AGO

"Look, Uncle Tom," cried Mary Jean.

She was out of breath from running up the hill. She could hardly talk.

Mr. North turned from the fence he had been fixing.

"Why, hello Mary Jean and Dick. What's all the excitement?"

Mr. North was Dick's father, and he was Mary Jean's uncle. Mary Jean lived in the city. She was visiting her uncle's farm.

"Well, Dad," Dick said, "Mary Jean wanted some more stones for her collection. I told her the best place to find them was along the brook. We were walking along the edge of the brook looking for stones when—"

Dick stopped. He, too, was out of breath from running up the hill.

"—when I found this," said Mary Jean. She held out her hand.

"What do you have?" Mr. North leaned over to take a closer look. "Why, it's an arrow head."

"That's what I thought," said Dick. "It was made by an Indian, wasn't it, Dad?"

Mr. North and Mary Jean and Dick were standing at the top of a hill. They could see for many miles.

"Everything you can see once belonged to the Indians," Mr. North said. "This land where our farm is belonged to the Indians at one time. Way over there, Mary Jean, is the city where you live. The land where the city now stands belonged to the Indians. All this and much, much more belonged to them. All of North America and South America belonged to them. That is thousands and thousands of miles."

"What did our country look like then?" asked Dick.

"It looked very different from the way it looks now. You know that little stretch of woods at the edge of our farm?" Mr. North pointed toward the woods.

"Oh, yes," said Mary Jean. "Dick and I have hiked through there. The trees and bushes are so thick that we could hardly walk. In some places the trees grow so close together that the sun cannot shine through."

"Well, that is only a very small woods," said Mr. North. "But this whole part of the country was one big woods, or forest, when the Indians lived here. At that time a squirrel could have traveled hundreds of miles through the trees without ever touching the ground."

North, "the Indians made arrow heads out of flint.

That is a very hard kind of stone. The Indians put the arrow heads on the ends of their arrows. They shot the arrows from bows. Bows and arrows were very important to the Indians, because they got most of their food and clothing by hunting. They did not have guns before the white men came."

"Were the Indians here a long time before the white men came, Uncle Tom?" asked Mary Jean.

"Yes. A long, long time. Nobody knows exactly how long."

5

"Whew!" exclaimed Dick. "Just think of that!"

"In other parts of the country there were not so many trees," said Mr. North. "There were deserts and grass-covered plains. But everywhere the country was almost the same as God made it. The Indians had not changed it. They had no big farms, no big cities, no roads. They loved the wilderness."

"The country has certainly changed since then," said Mary Jean. She looked out over the farms, the highways, the railroads, and the big city with its tall buildings and factories.

"Most of the people who built our country came from Europe, didn't they?" Dick asked.

"Yes," said Mr. North. "When we go into the house, I'll show you where it is on a map. It's about time to go in for lunch anyway."

Mr. North led Dick and Mary Jean to the room he called his den.

"I love maps," Mr. North said. "I have many of them. Let's see if I can find the right one. Ah, here it is."

Dick and Mary Jean looked on as Mr. North explained.

"The map shows where we think the first human beings lived. That place is in the western part of Asia. Adam and Eve and their children lived there. That was thousands and thousands of years ago. From there people spread over Asia, Europe, and Africa."

"Now over here," said Mr. North, "is the Holy Land. Our Lord lived and died here. That was about nineteen hundred years ago. While Our Lord was on earth He started His Church."

"That was the Catholic Church," said Dick.

Mr. North nodded. "Yes. The Catholic Church is the One True Church. It is the Church that was founded by God Himself. Well, the Apostles and other missionaries went out from the Holy Land. People in other parts of the world heard the missionaries. Many of these people became Catholics."

Mr. North pointed to the part of the map marked "Western Europe."

"Over here," he said, "is the western part of Europe. By the year 1000, almost everybody in Western Europe was a Catholic."

"What about America?" Mary Jean asked.

"I am coming to that. All this time, two great continents lay across the Atlantic Ocean. They were North America and South America. Nobody in Europe knew about North America and South America. Then in 1492 Christopher Columbus sailed from Europe. He sailed far across the Atlantic Ocean and discovered America. Later on, many people from Western Europe crossed the ocean to America. They built the United States. They also built the other countries on this side of the ocean."

"But the Indians were already here," said Dick. "How did they get here?"

"Was Columbus the first man from Europe to discover America?" asked Mary Jean. "Somebody told me that Leif Ericson was first."

"Why was Columbus sailing across the Atlantic if he did not know America was here?" Dick asked.

Mr. North laughed. "I hear Mother calling us for lunch, so I can't answer all your questions right now. Anyway, you will be going back to school next week. This year you are going to learn about the beginning of our country. I'm sure you will find the answers to these questions when you study history."

"I'll come back and visit you after we have been in school for a while," Mary Jean said. "Then Dick and I will let you know what we have found out."

"Fine," said Mr. North. "Do you still have the arrow head? Yes, I see you have. Don't lose it. Well, I'm hungry after my work."

"And we are hungry after our hike," said Dick.

"Then let's see what we have for lunch," said Mr. North.

"We are coming, Mother."

1. The Indians Were the First Americans

An Indian Family. This is an Indian family. The Indians lived in our country long before the white men came to America.

The family in this picture lived in the eastern part of our country. This part of the country was covered by a large forest. You can see many trees in the picture.

The father is bringing in a deer. He shot this deer with his bow and arrow. The Indian father is called a brave.

One of the boys is bringing in some fish which he caught in the river.

The mother is sitting by the fire. Indian wives are called squaws. This squaw is shelling corn. She raised this corn in a little field near the house. She will cook a piece of the deer. She will also cook the fish. Later, she will make clothes from the skin of the deer.

A baby is lying on the ground near the mother. An Indian baby is called a papoose.

The younger children are playing a game. Indian children love to play, as all children do.

Behind the mother you can see the house. It is made out of the bark of trees.

How the Indians Lived. You can see that the Indians did not live as we live today. They did not have big cities. They did not have big farms. They lived in the

1. The Indians Were the First Americans

Usually, a number of Indian families lived close to each other. These families formed a tribe. Each tribe had a chief, or leader. There were many wars between the tribes. Many people were killed in these bloody wars. When an Indian warrior killed an enemy it was the custom to cut off his head with an ax called a tomahawk. Then he would remove the hair, called the lock, and wear the clean scalp on his belt, like a medal. Indians loved to decorate themselves with paint and feathers before they went on the war path. When talking peace, the Indians sat in a circle and smoked the peace pipe.

wilderness. They got most of their food by hunting and fishing. They did not have roads like ours. Their only roads were trails through the forest. When Indians traveled, they either walked or went by canoe. They had no carts or wagons. They did not have horses until the white men came.

The Indians could not buy the things they needed. They had no stores. Each family made its own weapons, tools, and clothes. They made their weapons and tools out of wood, stone, and the bones of animals. They made their clothes out of the skins of animals. Instead of shoes they wore moccasins. For money they used shell beads called wampum.

The Indians did not know about the One True God. They worshiped the sun, the moon, the thunder, and many other things. Later the Catholic missionaries came and taught them about Our Lord. They also taught the Indians to love their fellow man.

Indians spoke many different languages. An Indian from one part of the country could not understand an Indian from another part of the country. For this reason, they sometimes used a sign language. They made certain signs with their hands. Each sign stood for a word or an idea. Most Indians could understand this sign language.

The Plains Indians. At the beginning of this chapter we read about an Indian family who lived in the eastern part of our country. This part of the country was covered by a great forest.

In the western part of our country there were many Indians who did not live in a forest. They lived on the plains. The plains were covered with thick grass, but they had very few trees. The Indians who lived here were called the Plains Indians.

Many animals fed on the grass of the plains. To the Indians, the most important of these animals was the buffalo, or bison.

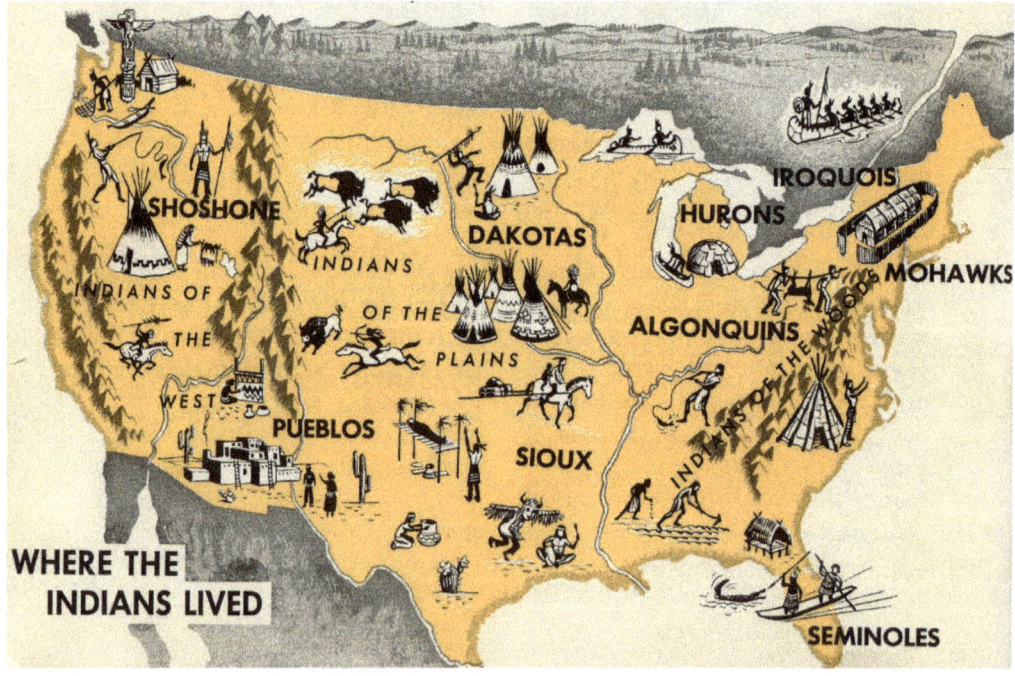

1. The Indians Were the First Americans

The Indians used the buffalo for many different purposes. They ate buffalo meat. They made clothes from buffalo skins. They made tepees, or wigwams, out of buffalo skins. They slept on beds made of buffalo skins. They even used buffalo skins to cover the framework of their boats.

The buffalo did not stay in one place very long. They moved about, looking for grass. The Indians followed them. Their tepees were easy to move. A tepee is really a tent. It has a frame made of sticks. A buffalo skin or deer skin is stretched over this frame. There is a hole in the top to let out smoke. There is an opening at the bottom which is used as a door.

The Indians of the Southwest. The Indians of the Southwest lived in big houses made of clay bricks. They were like apartment houses. These houses were called pueblos. Many families lived in one pueblo.

These Indians raised corn and many other vegetables. They made dishes and vases out of clay. They wove baskets from grass and other plants.

How Did the Indians Reach America? Most people think that the Indians probably came over to Alaska from Asia, but nobody knows for sure. On the map you can see that Alaska is very close to Asia. There is only a narrow strip of water, the Bering Strait, between Alaska and Asia. In winter this water freezes. Perhaps people from Asia walked across the ice to Alaska.

Or perhaps they came in canoes, in the summer.

These people probably built homes in Alaska. Later, some of their children or grandchildren may have moved south into Canada, later, some of the people no doubt moved farther south into the United States. Then some of them moved on to Mexico, Central America, and finally South America.

Why do we call these people Indians? We'll find the answer to that question in Chapter 6.

When the first white man came to America, there were Indians in almost every part of North America and South America.

The Indians really "discovered" America many hundreds of years before the white men did.

1. The Indians Were the First Americans

What We Have Received From the Indians. We have many things to remind us that the Indians were the first Americans. Many parts of our country have Indian names. A few of them are Ohio, Kentucky, Minnesota, Connecticut, and Mississippi. Many of our most important roads follow old Indian trails.

Today we use many plants which we learned about from the Indians. Here is a list of a few plants, fruits, and vegetables which the Indians taught the settler to cultivate: corn, beans, peanuts, tobacco, tomatoes, potatoes, sugar, and pumpkins. Indians taught their white friends to hunt, fish, and build canoes.

Study Lesson

WHAT AM I? Write each word and after it the phrase that explains it.

1. brave   2. tepee   3. pueblo
4. tribe   5. squaw   6. clay

a. an Indian wife.
b. an Indian hunter.
c. a group of Indians living close together.
d. Indian home built with clay bricks.
e. material used in making dishes.
f. home of the Plains Indians.

WHERE AM I? Answer each question in a complete sentence.

1. Where do most people believe the Indians lived before they came to North America?
2. In what part of the country did Indians live in clay brick houses?
3. Where did the Plains Indians live?
4. Can you name five places with Indian names?

WHAT IS THE REASON? Think carefully before you answer each question.

1. Why was the life of the Indian so different from ours?
2. Why did the Indian families make their own clothes and tools?
3. Why did the Indians worship the sun and other things?
4. Why was the buffalo so important to the Plains Indians?
5. Why did the Indians often use sign language?
6. What did the Indians teach their white friends?
7. How did we repay the Indians for their gifts to us?

WORDS TO KNOW. Use each of these words in a sentence. Look them up in your dictionary, or in the word list in the back of the book, if you are not sure of their meaning.

buffalo   **plains**   **deer**
moccasin **tomahawk** **papoose**
scalp   **wampum**   **lock**

2. The Northmen Find America

Northmen Were Good Sailors. The men in this boat are Northmen. The brave Northmen lived in the northern part of Europe about a thousand years ago. They lived in Norway, Sweden, and Denmark.

The Northmen were tall and sturdy. Their skin was light and their hair was blond. They were good fighters and good sailors. They sailed in boats like the one in the picture.

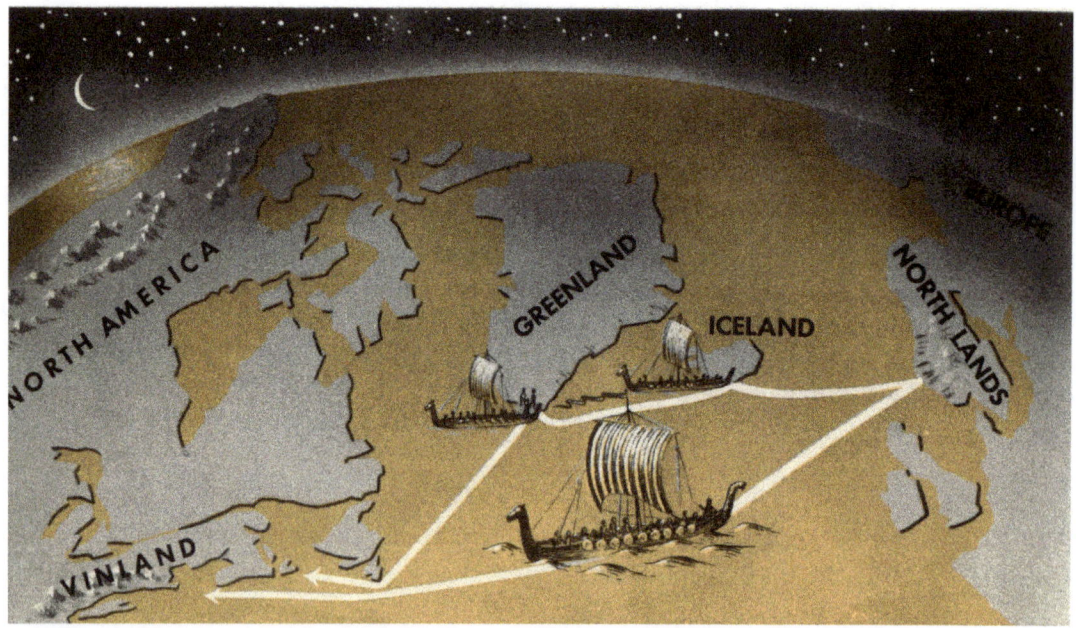

2. The Northmen Find America

Leif, the Son of Eric. About 986 some Northmen moved from Iceland to Greenland. The leader of these Northmen was Eric the Red. As you can see on the map, Greenland is an island near North America.

Eric the Red did not know that he was living close to North America. He did not even know that there was such a place as North America.

Eric had a son named Leif. He was called Leif Ericson. This means "Leif, son of Eric." Leif was only two years old when his family moved from Iceland to Greenland.

you can see, there is the head of a dragon on the front of the boat. The boat is painted black. It has both a sail and oars. The boat would look very small if it were put next to one of our great steamships of today. Yet the Northmen sailed hundreds of miles in little boats like this. They traveled on the ocean close to Europe. They sailed up the rivers of Europe.

About the year 860 some daring Northmen sailed out over the ocean. They did not see land for many days. At last they came to an island which they named Iceland. Iceland is between Europe and America. You can see it on the map.

After that, many Northmen went to Iceland. They took their families with them. They built homes and lived there.

Leif heard many stories about Norway. He knew that the first Northmen who came to Iceland were from Norway. His own father, Eric the Red, was born there. Leif decided that he would like to visit Norway. Like all Northmen, he was a good sailor. In the year 999 he sailed to Norway. He was nineteen years old.

Leif Becomes a Catholic. King Olaf of Norway was happy to see Leif. He invited Leif to spend the winter with him.

King Olaf had become a Catholic. He told Leif about the One True God. Leif listened with great interest. He had never heard about the One True God. The Northmen in Iceland and Greenland worshiped many false gods.

Before the winter was over, Leif became a Catholic. Then he could hardly wait to get back to Greenland. He wanted to tell his mother and father and everyone else in Greenland about the Catholic religion. King Olaf sent two priests with Leif when he started back to Greenland.

Leif Visits America. Leif sailed too far south. He missed Greenland. For days, Leif and his men saw nothing but water. How happy they must have been when they finally saw land.

But Leif knew that this land was not Greenland. This land was covered by a great forest, but there were few trees in Greenland.

The men got off the boat and looked around. They found wildwheat. They also found many vines with grapes on

2. The Northmen Find America

Leif About to Land in North America

when they went back to their boats to sail home to Greenland. They also took some dried grapes. The people of Greenland were happy to get these things. There was little lumber in Greenland. Grapes do not grow there at all. Greenland is too far north.

Leif brought the people of Greenland a gift more valuable than grapes or lumber. That gift was the True Faith. From Leif and the two priests from Norway, Greenlanders learned about Our Lord and His Church. Most of the people became Catholics. Churches were built. Before many years there was even a bishop in Greenland.

Vinland Is Forgotten. The people of Greenland were interested in Leif's story about Vinland. About 150 men, women, and children moved to North America. A baby girl was born to one of the families. She was probably the first white child born in North America. The girl's name was Snorri.

them. Grapes are used to make wine, so Leif named the country Vinland. This means Wineland.

Where is the country that Leif Ericson named Vinland? We do not know for sure. It may have been Nova Scotia. Or it may have been New England. Anyway, we are quite sure that it was in North America.

Leif Ericson and his Northmen were probably the first white men to see North America. This happened in the year 1000.

Leif Returns to Greenland. Leif and his men took some lumber with them

The settlers had trouble with the Indians. They also had other troubles. Finally, they gave up and sailed back to Greenland.

During the next 250 years the Northmen sometimes sailed to Vinland to get lumber. They did not try to build homes there. After a while they stopped visiting Vinland. They almost forgot that there was such a place.

Most of the people of Europe never heard about Leif's discovery. They did not even know that there was land on the other side of Greenland. They called the Atlantic Ocean the "Sea of Darkness" because they did not know what was on the other side. Most sailors in Europe were afraid to sail out very far on the ocean. They did not want to get out of sight of land.

Leif Ericson was a great sailor and a very brave man. He sailed across the ocean and discovered America about 500 years before anyone else did. But nothing came of his discovery.

In 1492 America was to be discovered again, by another man from Europe. This discovery was to be more important. It caused many people to cross the ocean from Europe and make their homes in America. We shall read about this discovery in Chapter 6.

2. The Northmen Find America

STUDY LESSON

WHO AM I? Write the name of each of the persons listed below. Then write the sentence which tells you about each person.

1. King Olaf   2. Snorri
3. Leif Ericson   4. Eric the Red

a. I led the Northmen to Greenland.
b. I discovered Vinland by accident.
c. I taught Leif Ericson about the Catholic religion.
d. I was probably the first white child born in America.

WHAT AM I? Write each word and after it the phrase that explains it.

1. sailor   2. lumber   3. settlers   4. true religion

a. They had trouble with the Indians in Vinland.
b. Leif Ericson was one of these by trade.
c. People sailed from Greenland to Vinland for it.
d. Priests brought it to the people in Greenland.

DATES TO REMEMBER. First write the dates in column A. Next to each one write the sentence from column B that matches each date.

A	B
860	a. The first Northmen reach North America.
1000	b. Iceland is discovered.

SOMETHING TO THINK ABOUT. Think carefully before you answer these questions.

1. Why was Leif Ericson's trip to Norway so important?
2. Why did only a few people from Europe come to America after its discovery by Leif Ericson?
3. Why did the Norse settlers leave Vinland?
4. Why were the people in Greenland interested in Leif's story about Vinland?
5. How did King Olaf help to spread the Catholic religion?

WHERE IS THIS? Next to each place write the sentence locating it.

1. Iceland   2. Norway   3. Europe
4. Vinland   5. Greenland

a. Olaf ruled here.
b. This land may have been New England.
c. The first island the Northmen reached was between Europe and America.
d. The Northmen sailed up the rivers of this region.
e. Few trees grew on this bare island.

WORDS TO KNOW. Use each of these words in a sentence. Use your dictionary if you are not sure what they mean.

Northmen   **valuable**
dragon   **lumber**

3. The Holy Wars

John Goes Off to War. John is saying goodbye to his mother and father and to his sisters and brothers. It is the year 1096. John is going to leave his home in Europe. He is going off to war. This is a very important war.

"I'll be back after we rescue the Holy Land from the Turks," John says.

"Goodbye, my son," says his father, "God bless you and protect you."

As John goes off, he wonders what kind of adventures he will have. He wonders what sights he will see.

John has never been more than fifteen miles from his own home.

He does not know very much about the rest of the world. The other members of his family do not know very much about the rest of the world either. Neither do the other people in his village.

In those days most people who lived in Europe did very little traveling. They spent their whole lives in the place where they were born. They could not read about the other parts of the world because there were very few books. Printing had not been invented. Very few people learned to read.

So you can see why John was excited as he set off on his long journey to the Holy Land.

3. The Holy Wars

Why John Went to War. Why was John going off to war? If you will look at the map, you will see the Holy Land. It is in the part of the world we call the Near East.

The biggest city in the Holy Land is Jerusalem.

Our Lord was born in the Holy Land. He spent most of his life there. He died there, and He was buried there. The Catholic Church had its start in the Holy Land. From there, the Apostles carried the Faith to Europe and other places.

Catholics love to visit the Holy Land. They like to kneel and pray at the spots where Our Lord was born, where He died, and where He was buried.

The Turks had captured the Holy Land. The Turks were not Catholics. They hated the Catholic religion. The Turks spoiled many Catholic churches in the Holy Land. They robbed and killed Catholics who visited the Holy Land.

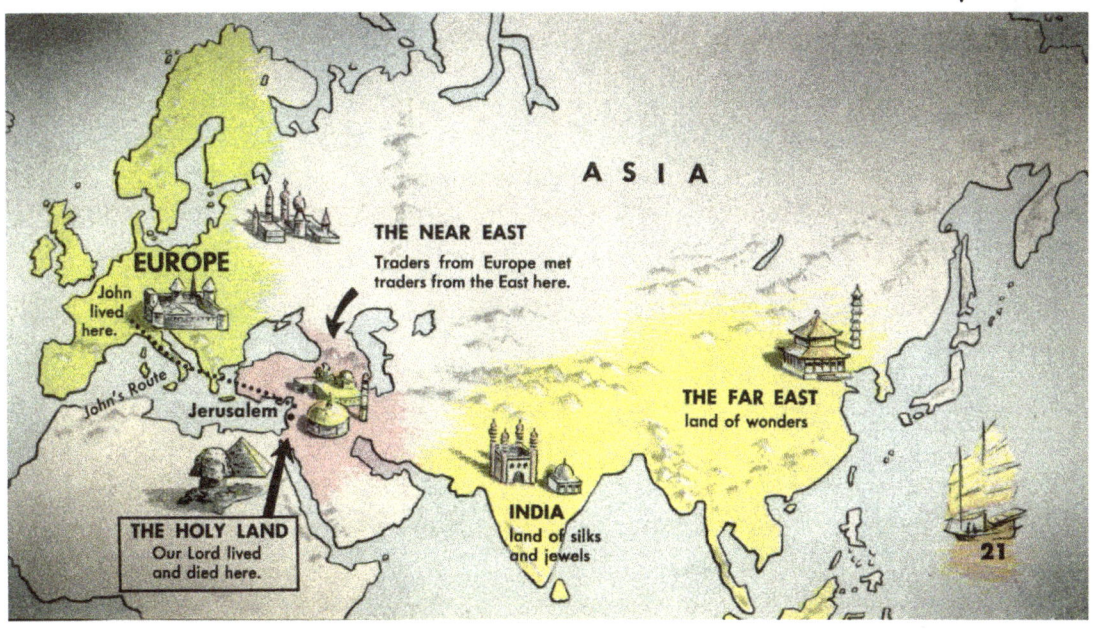

In 1095 the Pope asked the people of Europe to rescue the Holy Land from the Turks. In those days almost everybody in Europe was a Catholic. The men of Europe were happy to do what the Pope asked. So the next year, thousands of soldiers from Europe marched off to fight in this Holy War. The Holy War was called a Crusade. The soldiers were called Crusaders. The word Crusade means marked with a cross. The soldiers wore Our Lord's Cross on their shields.

John was one of the Crusaders. In the picture at the beginning of this chapter you can see the Cross on his cloak.

As you see, John had a sword and shield. The Crusaders did not have guns. Guns had not yet been invented. Some of the Crusaders rode horses, but John was too poor to buy a horse. He traveled in the company of nobles and poor village people.

Now, we shall read about John's adventures.

3. The Holy Wars

John Sees Wonderful Sights. John and the other Crusaders marched for many months. John was often tired and hungry and thirsty.

At last the Crusaders reached the Near East. Here John saw many wonderful sights.

He saw cities that were many times as big as his little village at home. He saw houses that were much better than his little cottage. He saw beautiful churches. He saw the Mediterranean Sea and was surprised that there could be so much water in the world. He saw a great sandy desert. When he saw his first camel, John said, "What a strange-looking animal. Wait till I tell the people at home about this. They will hardly believe it."

John Visits the Markets. John's eyes opened wide with wonder when he visited a market in the Near East. He saw many wonderful things that he had never seen before. There were beautiful rugs, silks, emeralds, pearls, china.

"Where do all these things come from?" he asked the Arab who owned the market.

"From lands thousands of miles to the east," the Arab merchant answered. "They are brought here by camel train."

The map on page 19 shows what the Arab meant. Most of the goods came from that part of the world which we call the Far East.

John was in the Near East, but he was looking at goods which came from the Far East.

"What are they for?" John asked.

"They make food taste better."

John thought of the very plain food they had at home. Every meal was bread and meat. All the meals tasted the same. It would be wonderful if he could make the meat taste better.

"I'll buy some spices," John said. "I want to take them home with me."

The Crusaders Take Jerusalem. When they had reached the Holy Land the Crusaders fought many battles with the Turks. The Turks were fierce fighters. Many of John's friends were wounded. Some of them were killed. In 1099 the Crusaders captured the city of Jerusalem.

John knelt at the spot where Our Lord had been buried.

"Thank you, dear Lord," he said, "for keeping me safe to see this holy spot."

John Buys Some Spice. Before John left the market he pointed to some boxes.

"What is in those boxes?" he asked.

"Spices," the Arab answered. "Pepper, nutmeg, cloves, cinnamon, and many other spices."

John Returns Home. You can imagine how happy John's family were to see him when he came back home. He had been away for five years.

"Thank you, God, for bringing our son safe home," John's mother prayed when she saw him.

Eagerly they listened to the story of John's adventures. They were interested in the sights that he had seen. Then John told them about the wonderful things he had seen in the markets of the East. He showed them the spices he had bought there. He told them how tasty they would make the food.

"I'll try the spices when I cook dinner today," John's mother said.

When they were eating dinner, John's father said: "This is the best meal I have ever tasted. I wish we could buy more spices."

"Perhaps we will soon be able to buy spices right here in Europe," John said. "Perhaps many of the other wonders that I saw in the Eastern markets will be sold near home, too. All the Crusaders are coming home and telling about these things. People all over Europe will soon want to buy them, and they will find a way."

John was right. In the Italian cities of Venice and Genoa there were many wealthy merchants. Merchants are men who buy and sell. These merchants sent their ships to the Near East. The ships came back loaded with new goods. The merchants soon were shipping these things to markets all over Europe.

The new goods were very expensive when they reached Europe. John's father could not afford to buy many spices for every day use. But he was glad that he could buy some to use in special dishes around the holidays.

The Holy Wars Changed Life in Europe. The Crusaders were not able to keep Jerusalem. The Turks captured the city again. There were more Crusades after the first one. The Crusades lasted about 200 years. At the end of that time the Turks still held the Holy Land.

The Holy Wars were very important even though the Crusaders were not able to hold the Holy Land. The wars caused the people of Europe to become more interested in other parts of the world. The wars also caused the people of Europe to get used to buying many goods from the Far East.

About 200 years later a man tried to find a new route to use in bringing the goods from the Far East. Instead of finding the Far East on this route, he discovered America. That man was Christopher Columbus.

So, we see that the Holy Wars helped lead to the discovery of America.

3. THE HOLY WARS

STUDY LESSON

WHERE IS IT? Write the name of each place listed below. Next to it write the sentence which tells you about it.

    1. Europe   2. Far East
    3. Jerusalem   4. Venice
    5. Near East   6. Mediterranean

a. This is the largest city in the Holy Land.
b. The Holy Land was in this part of the world.
c. John's home was in this part of the world.
d. Merchants from this city sent their ships to the Near East.
e. Crusaders crossed this sea to reach the Holy Land.
f. Spices came from this part of the East.

WHAT AM I? Write each word and after it the phrase that explains it.

    1. spices 2. Crusader 3. merchants
    4. Turks 5. Crusade

a holy war.
b. a soldier who fought to free the Holy Land.
c. fierce fighters who lived in the Near East
d. pepper and cloves and other things used to make food tastier.
e. men who buy and sell things.

SOMETHING TO THINK ABOUT. Think carefully before you answer each question.

1. Why did Christians come to visit the Holy Land?
2. Why didn't people in Europe at the time of the Crusades know much about the world?
3. Why did the Crusaders go to the Holy Land?
4. Why did John want to bring spices home?
5. How did the Holy Wars change life in Europe?
6. How did the Crusades lead to the discovery of America?
7. Does the Church have any enemies today? What is the best way of fighting them?

WORDS TO KNOW. Use each of these words in a sentence. Use your dictionary if you are not sure what they mean.

adventure   **market**   **printing**

cinnamon   **desert**   **fierce**

4. Marco Polo Visits the Far East

Marco Sees the Great Khan. Marco Polo lived in the city of Venice. His father and uncle were merchants in that city.

By 1271 the Crusades were over. Then Marco and his father and his uncle started out on a trip. They were going to visit the Great Khan. The Great Khan ruled China and other parts of the Far East.

Marco Polo was only seventeen years old when he started on the trip. This young man was going to do something that few people from Europe had ever done. He was going to visit the Far East.

The people of Europe were using many goods from the Far East, but very few of them had ever seen the Far East.

The Polos traveled by ship to the eastern end of the Mediterranean Sea. Now they were in the Near East. They still had a long, long way to go before they reached the Far East. They used camels to cross the desert. They used burros to cross the mountains. They used horses to cross the plains. It took the Polos almost four years to reach the palace where the Great Khan lived in China.

4. Marco Polo Visits the Far East

Marco could hardly believe his eyes when he saw the great palace. It was made of marble. It was decorated with gold and precious jewels. It was rich in carpets and fine furniture. Marco had never seen anything like it before in his life.

In the picture, you can see Marco meeting the Great Khan in his palace.

Marco Works for the Khan. The Great Khan liked Marco Polo. He asked Marco to work for him. He asked Marco to travel through the Far East and tell him what he saw. Marco traveled thousands of miles. He learned to speak several languages. He saw many many wonderful sights. After each trip he told the Great Khan about the things he had seen and the people he had visited.

Marco saw cities that were bigger than any cities in Europe. He saw the Pacific Ocean. He saw people riding on elephants. In China he saw people burning coal to keep warm. Marco had never seen coal before. It looked like stone to him. He said that the people

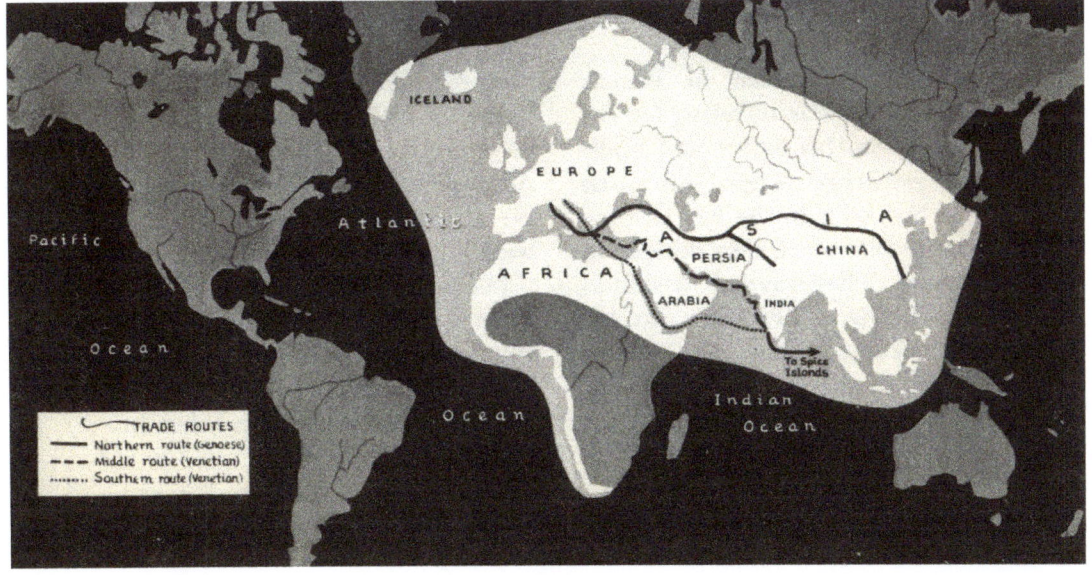

were burning black stones. That was a mistake.

Marco Polo found that the people of the Far East had the finest carpets in the world. They had beautiful silk cloth. They had all kinds of precious stones. In Europe these things were very expensive, but in the Far East they did not cost very much.

The Polos Return to Venice. While Marco was traveling for the Great Khan, his father and uncle were gathering riches. After the Polos had been in the Far East for about twenty years, they decided to go home. They traveled by ship as far as Persia. Then they traveled by camel to the Black Sea. There they got on another ship and sailed to Venice. They had been away for twenty-four years on their travels.

The people of Venice were amazed when they saw the costly jewels and other beautiful things which the Polos had brought back from the Far East. They loved to hear the Polos tell about their travels.

Marco Writes a Book. After Marco Polo returned to Venice there was a war between his city and the city of Genoa. Marco was captured. He was put into a prison in Genoa. While he was in prison he wrote a book about his travels. After printing was invented, people all over Europe read Marco's book.

Many people had the same idea when they read Marco's book. This was what they thought: "Marco Polo says that spices, precious stones, and other goods cost much less in the Far East than they do in Europe. But it is no wonder they cost so much in Europe. The goods have

4. Marco Polo Visits the Far East

to travel thousands of miles by camel train before they are put on a ship. It costs more to send goods by land than by water. Marco Polo, tells us that there is an ocean in the Far East. If we could find a way to sail ships to the Far East on that ocean we could bring the goods back by water. Then they would not cost us so much."

One of the men who tried to find a way to sail ships to the Far East was Prince Henry of Portugal. We shall read about him in the next chapter.

STUDY LESSON

WHERE IS IT? Write the name of each place listed below. Next to it write the fact which tells you about it.

1. Pacific 2. China 3. Genoa
4. Venice 5. Persia

a. While he was in the Far East, Marco Polo saw this great ocean.
b. On their way home the Polos traveled as far as this country by ship.
c. The Polos had been away from this city for twenty-four years.
d. Marco Polo was put in prison in this city.
e. The Great Khan was ruler of this country.

WHAT AM I? Write each word and after it the phrase that explains it.

1. burros 2. marble 3. coal

a. what Marco saw the Chinese using for heat
b. the animals used by the Polos to cross mountains
c. material for the Great Khan's palace

SOMETHING TO THINK ABOUT. Think carefully before you answer these questions.

1. Why did it take the Polos so long to reach China?
2. Why did Marco Polo learn so much about the Far East?
3. Why were the people of Venice amazed at the return of the Polos from the Far East?
4. Why was Marco Polo put in prison?
5. Why were people all over Europe able to read Marco Polo's book?
6. Why did some of the people who read Marco Polo's book want to send ships all the way to the Far East?

WORDS TO KNOW. Use each of these words in a sentence. Look them up in your dictionary if you are not sure of their meaning.

expensive	**amazed**
jewels	**carpets**
prison	**precious**

5. Prince Henry's Sailors

Prince Henry Starts a School. The man in this picture is Prince Henry of Portugal. Prince Henry is teaching school. His pupils are not boys and girls. They are grown men. They are sailors.

What is Prince Henry saying to the sailors? Let's listen.

"I want you to look at this map," Prince Henry says. "Here is Portugal." He points to his own country. "And here is the Far East." He points again.

"Our country is on an ocean," Prince Henry says. "And Marco Polo says there is also an ocean in the Far East. Now I feel sure that there is some way to sail a ship from Portugal to the Far East. We know we can't go by way of the Mediterranean Sea. The Isthmus of Suez blocks the way."

The sailors listen with interest to what the Prince is saying.

"So here is my idea," Prince Henry says. "I think the only way we can get

5. Prince Henry's Sailors

a ship to the Far East is to sail around Africa."

The sailors look at each other. Some of them are frightened.

"I know what you are thinking," Prince Henry says. "Nobody has ever sailed very far down the coast of Africa. You have heard all kinds of stories about the dangers in that part of the world. You have heard that the ocean is boiling hot. You have heard about terrible monsters who would destroy ships."

The sailors nod. They have heard these things. They have also heard many other terrible things about that part of the world.

"Well, I don't believe those stories," Prince Henry says. "Besides, you are very brave men. That is why I chose you to come to this school."

The sailors smile. They are glad the Prince thinks they are brave.

"Before you start sailing down the coast of Africa there are many things you must learn," Prince Henry says. "You must learn to use the compass. You must learn to read the stars. You must learn how to make maps and charts. That is why I have started this school."

NEW HELPS FOR SAILORS

We have read that the people of Europe were trying to find a way to the Far East. About this time other changes took place in Europe. These changes helped the men who were sailing ships farther and farther from home. Here are some of the changes:

JOHN GUTENBERG

Before John Gutenberg invented a new way to print books about 1450, all books were printed by hand. Sailors could not write about the things they had seen on their trips because it took too much time to write books. When John Gutenberg invented movable type and the printing press, books could be easily printed. Now sailors could write about what they had seen. Other sailors would know what to expect when visiting strange lands. Many people could now own books who before could not afford to buy them. In this way, knowledge spread widely throughout the world.

THE ASTROLABE

To help a captain know exactly where he was on the ocean, the astrolabe and clock were invented. The astrolabe told sailors how far north or south of the equator their ship was. The clock helped captains to figure out how far north or south they had sailed. Both these inventions were related to the positions of certain stars. Without the astrolabe and the compass, America would have remained unknown for many centuries.

THE COMPASS

When the compass was invented, sailors no longer had to fear getting lost. The compass showed them in what direction they were sailing. With the compass they could sail farther than ever before.

GUNPOWDER

While learning about printing, the astrolabe, the clock, and the compass, Europeans also found out about gunpowder. Sailors landing in strange lands now protected themselves with gunpowder.

5. Prince Henry's Sailors

Why Prince Henry Wished to Find the Far East. There were two reasons why Prince Henry wished to sail his ships to the Far East.

Here is the first reason: Prince Henry loved his country. He wanted the ships of his country to bring the goods from the Far East to Europe. This would make Portugal rich and powerful.

Here is the second reason: Prince Henry was a very good Catholic. He knew that the people of the Far East were pagans. They did not know about Our Lord and His Church. Prince Henry wanted to send priests to the Far East. He wanted the people of the Far East to learn about the True Church.

Prince Henry's Sailors Go Farther and Farther. Prince Henry's sailors took their ships farther and farther down the coast of Africa. When a captain decided to turn around and go back home he had his men build a stone tower on the coast. Then the next ship would go past this tower. The men on this ship would build another tower. Each ship was supposed to go a little farther than the one before it.

Prince Henry died in 1460. By then, his sailors had gone as far as Cape Verde. Find Cape Verde on the map. This was much farther than any people from Europe had ever gone before by ship.

When Prince Henry died, he was sure that his plan would work. He was sure that some day a sailor from Portugal would go all the way around Africa and on to the Far East. Twenty-six years after Prince Henry's death, his dream came true.

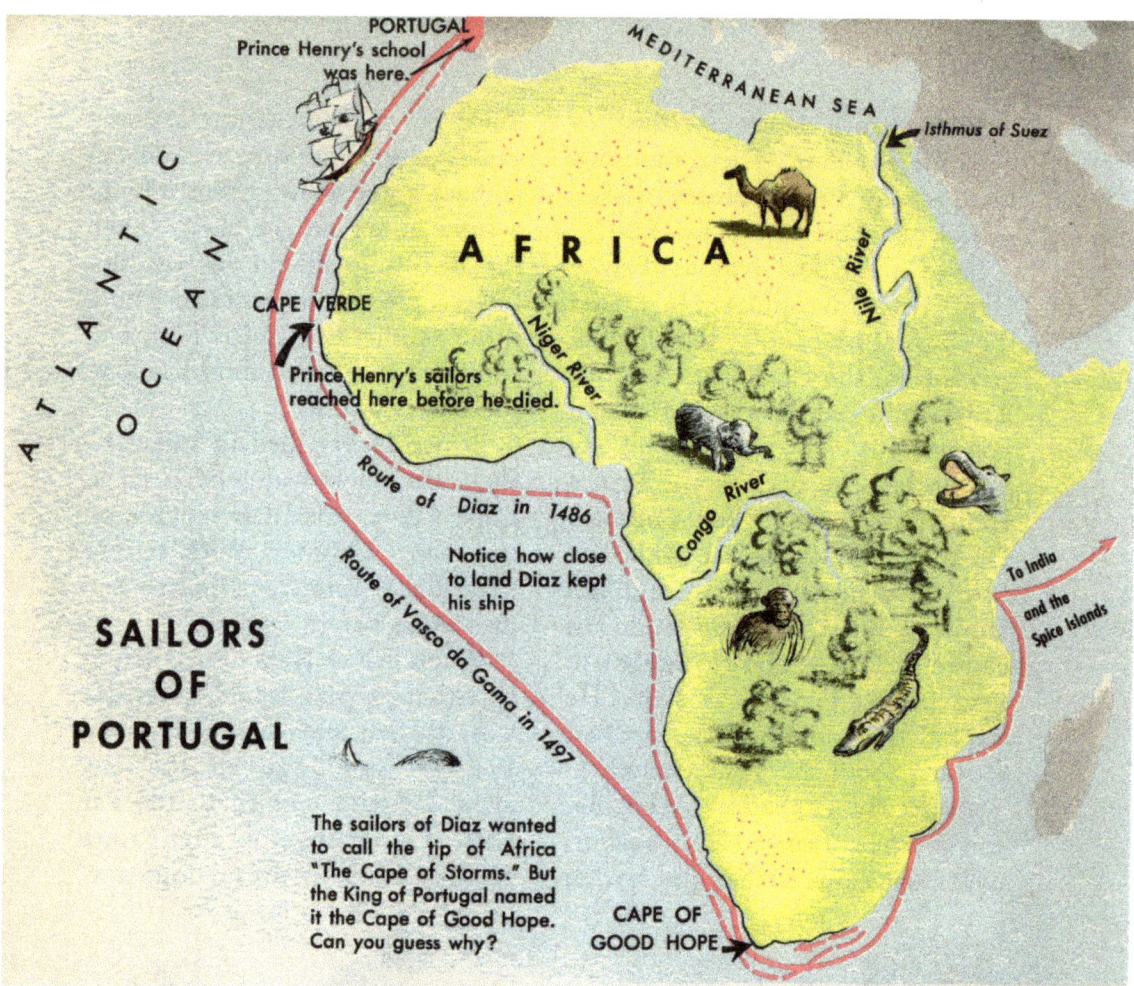

Diaz Finds the Tip of Africa. The sailors from Portugal did not give up after Prince Henry died. They kept going farther and farther down the coast of Africa. Sometimes they felt like giving up. It seemed that they could never reach the tip of Africa. They did not know, of course, that Africa is the second largest of all the continents. Small wonder the trip took so long.

At last, in 1486, Bartholomeu Diaz reached the southern tip of Africa. He sailed around the tip. Then he went back and told the good news to the King of Portugal.

King John of Portugal was happy. Now he knew that it was possible to sail around Africa. He was so happy that he named the tip of Africa the Cape of Good Hope.

5. Prince Henry's Sailors

Prince Henry had been right. It was possible to sail around Africa.

Twelve years later in 1498 a ship from Portugal sailed around Africa and reached the Far East. That was six years after Columbus had discovered America.

STUDY LESSON

WHO AM I? Write the name of each of the following persons. Next to each name, write the sentence which tells you about the person.

   1. King John   2. Prince Henry
   3. Bartholomeu Diaz   4. Gutenberg

a. I ran a school for sailors.
b. I first sailed around the tip of Africa.
c. I named the tip of Africa the Cape of Good Hope.
d. I am called the "Father of Printing."

WHERE IS IT? Write the name of each of the following places. Next to each write the sentence which tells about it.

   1. Isthmus of Suez   2. Cape Verde
   3. Portugal   4. Africa

a. Prince Henry lived here.
b. The Portuguese sailors did not know that this was the second largest of all the continents.
c. Part of Africa reached by the Portuguese before Prince Henry died.
d. This strip of land blocked the way to the Far East by water.

SOMETHING TO THINK ABOUT. Think carefully before answering these questions.

1. Why did Prince Henry want to send sailors around the tip of Africa?
2. Why did Prince Henry want to send ships to the Far East?
3. Why was the tip of Africa named the Cape of Good Hope?
4. Why were the sailors afraid of sailing down the coast of Africa?
5. Why do you think that the Portuguese sailors finally succeeded?
6. Why did Prince Henry run a school for sailors?

DATES TO REMEMBER. Write the dates in column A. Then next to each one write the sentence from column B that matches it.

A	B
1486	Gutenberg lived at this time.
1450	Diaz sailed around the tip of Africa.

WORDS TO KNOW. Use each of these words in a sentence. Look them up in your dictionary if you are not sure of their meaning.

   isthmus   **ocean**   **compass**

6. Christopher Columbus Discovers America

Columbus Becomes a Sailor. Christopher Columbus was born in the city of Genoa about 1446. Genoa was an exciting city to live in. As you know, the merchants of Genoa used to send ships to the Near East. The ships would come back to Genoa with all sorts of wonderful goods. Then other ships carried these goods out of Genoa to all parts of Europe.

When Columbus was a boy he watched the ships come and go. He saw sailors taking beautiful rugs and silks and other goods off the ships. He watched them put these goods on other ships. Often Christopher talked with the sailors. They told him about the strange lands they had seen. They told about their adventures. Christopher longed to be a sailor.

6. Christopher Columbus Discovers America

When Christopher Columbus was fourteen years old, his wish came true. In the picture above you see young Christopher Columbus working on board a ship. The ships of those days were quite different from the great ships of today. The steamship had not been invented. All the ships had sails. They could move only when the wind was blowing. The ships were also very small.

Columbus Visits Portugal. When he grew up, Columbus lived for awhile in the city of Lisbon. Lisbon is in Portugal. Can you find Lisbon on the map?

Columbus learned much while he was in Lisbon.

Prince Henry had died before Columbus came to Portugal. But sailors from Portugal were still trying to sail around Africa.

Columbus talked to these sailors. He learned many things from them. He learned how to make maps while he was in Portugal. He learned to speak Portuguese and Spanish. He learned how to read Latin. Many important books were printed in Latin.

Columbus Has an Idea. Columbus read the book which Marco Polo had written about his travels. He also read many other books about the world. Some of the books were in handwriting. Others were printed. Printing had been invented about the time Columbus was born.

As Columbus read, his mind was busy, too. This is what he thought. "Almost all wise men say the earth is round. If that is so, then it should be possible to reach the Far East by sailing to the West. The sailors of Portugal are trying to reach the Far East by sailing around Africa.

Wouldn't it be better to sail out across the Atlantic Ocean?"

Columbus Tries to Get Help. Columbus was sure his idea was right. He wanted to try it. But Columbus had no money. He could not hire sailors or buy ships.

For many years Columbus tried to find somebody who would help him. He asked the King of Portugal for help. Columbus's brother asked the kings of England and France for help. But these kings would not help him. Few people had ever sailed very far out on the Atlantic Ocean. Even the sailors from Portugal who were trying to reach the Far East stayed close to the coast of Africa. The kings were afraid that something might happen to Columbus if he sailed too far out on the ocean. They were afraid he and his ships would never come back.

Columbus went to Spain. He wished to ask the King and Queen of Spain to help him. He arrived there at a bad time. The Spaniards were at war with the Moors. The war was costing a great deal of money. The King and Queen did not see how they could help Columbus while the war was going on. Columbus decided to leave Spain. He took his son, Diego, and they headed toward France.

Diego got hungry on the trip, so Columbus stopped at a monastery for something to eat. That was the custom in those days. There were no roadhouse restaurants then. At the monastery Columbus met Father Juan Perez. He told Father Perez about his plan. Father Perez liked the plan. He knew Queen Isabella well. He said he would talk to her about Columbus and his plan to sail across the Atlantic Ocean to reach India.

After Queen Isabella talked with Father Perez she said she would like to see Columbus again. Soon she agreed to help Columbus.

At last Columbus was able to make his voyage.

The Great Voyage. Columbus had three ships and about ninety men. On the morning of August 3, 1492 the men went to Mass and received Holy Communion. Father Perez blessed the men and the ships. He asked God to protect the little

6. Christopher Columbus Discovers America

fleet. Then the men got on the ships and sailed out of the harbor.

Christopher Columbus was on the largest of the three ships. It was named the *Santa Maria*, in honor of the Blessed Mother. These words mean "St. Mary." The other two ships were called the *Nina* and the *Pinta*.

Day after day passed, and there was no sight of land. The sailors became frightened. They were afraid that perhaps the world was flat and they might sail off the edge. They were afraid there might be terrible monsters in the water. They were afraid if they went too far they might never be able to find their way home again.

The men begged Columbus to turn around and go back to Spain. Columbus would not do it. He had waited for years for his chance. He would not give up now. He told his men to sail on. He prayed to God for help. Every evening he had his men sing a hymn to the Blessed Mother. This is how God answered his prayers.

Land, at Last! On the night of October 11, Columbus was standing on the deck of the Santa Maria. As he looked out over the dark water, he thought he saw a light. Did this mean that there was land ahead? He thought so, but he could not be sure.

At two o'clock the next morning, a sailor on the Pinta saw in the moonlight a dark line of land.

"Land! Land!" the sailer shouted.

The men on the other ships heard the cry. They ran to the decks to look. They, too, saw the land.

"Land! Land!" they shouted with joy.

Columbus asked his men to sing a hymn of thanksgiving to God. They thanked Him for guiding them safely over the vast ocean and bringing them to land at last.

A New World Is Discovered. In the morning Columbus dressed in his best clothes. He led his men ashore. They knelt on the ground and thanked God for their safe voyage. Then Columbus said that the land he had discovered belonged to the King and Queen of Spain. He named

the land San Salvador. This means "Holy Saviour."

The land which Columbus found was an island in the Bahamas. You can see the Bahamas on the map on the next page. These islands are close to North America. They are also close to South America. Columbus did not know he was close to North America and South America because nobody in Europe knew about America. Columbus thought he was in the Far East.

Columbus had made a great discovery, but he did not know it. He had discovered land in the Western Hemisphere. Before long this land was to be called the New World.

There were people living on this island. Columbus thought he was near India, so he called the people Indians. Ever since then, the copper-colored people of America have been called Indians. Now you can answer the question that was asked in Chapter 1. Now you know how the Indians got their name.

Columbus Returns to Spain. Columbus sailed about among the islands. He was puzzled. He did not see the great cities that Marco Polo had written about. He did not see any beautiful rugs or silks. He did not see marble palaces or beautiful clothes. The Indians lived in huts and were poorly dressed.

Columbus sailed back to Spain. He took some Indians with him. He also

took some parrots and other birds and animals. He took a few gold ornaments that he had bought from the Indians. When he returned to Spain he was greeted as a great hero. Everyone was sure that he had found a way to sail to the Far East. King Ferdinand and Queen Isabella were glad they had helped Columbus make his journey.

Columbus made three more voyages to the New World. He saw the coast of South America and the coast of Central America. He was still puzzled because he found no great riches.

Why the Voyage of Columbus Was Important. Columbus died in 1506. He was puzzled and disappointed in his last years. He was sure that he had reached the Far East, but he could not understand why he had not found any riches. He did not know that he had found a greater and richer New World. How little he knew of its size, fine climate, and rich soil!

We know that Christopher Columbus was not the first person to find America. The Indians had been there for thousands of years. Leif Eriscon and the Northmen found America almost 500 years before Columbus did.

But the Indians did very little to change America. America was a wilderness when the Indians came, and

6. Christopher Columbus Discovers America

it was still the same wilderness when Columbus landed.

The Northmen did not stay very long in America. Few people in Europe even heard about their discovery until much later.

Everybody in Europe heard about the voyage of Christopher Columbus. Later many people from Europe crossed the ocean to America. They built homes, farms, cities, and roads. In time, they formed many new nations. One of these nations was the United States of America.

Da Gama Reaches the Far East. In 1498 a captain from Portugal made Prince Henry's dream come true. This was just six years after Columbus had

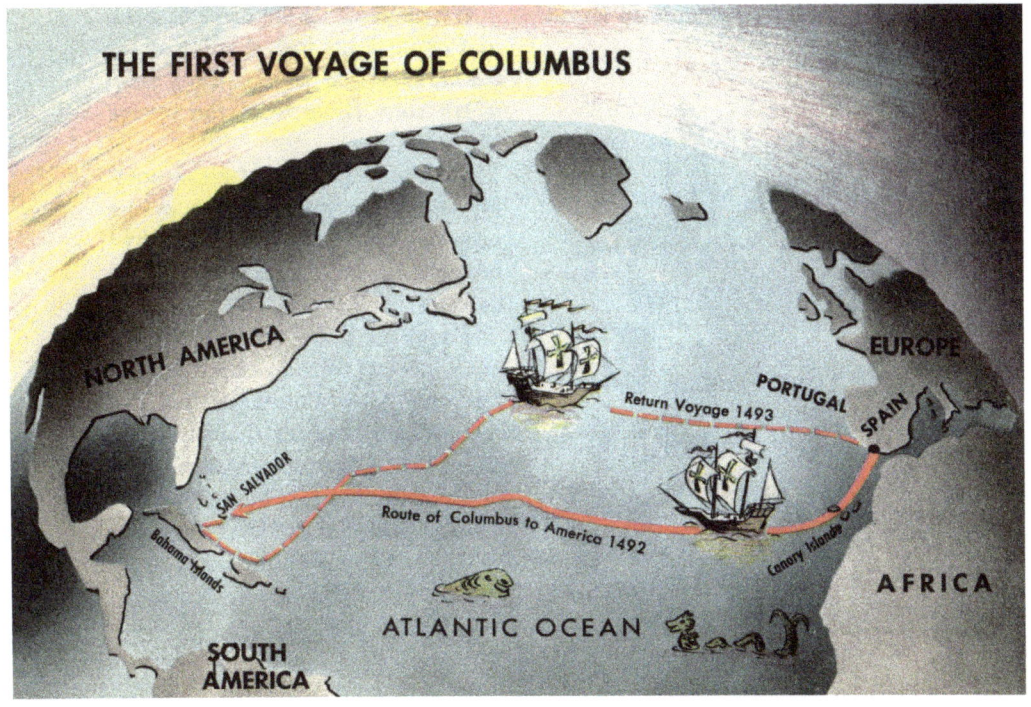

discovered America. The captain's name was Vasco da Gama. Da Gama sailed all the way around Africa. Then he sailed on to India. At last someone had found a new route to the Far East. It was a great day for Portugal's merchants.

More than that it was a great day for the missions. When Vasco da Gama found his new route to the East he made it possible for St. Francis Xavier to bring the Catholic Faith to the people in India.

When Vasco da Gama came back to Portugal he had a shipload of spices, silks, and jewels. They were worth sixty times what the voyage had cost.

Da Gama became a great hero. He seemed a greater hero to the people than Columbus. He had brought back riches but Columbus had not.

Today we know why the voyages of Columbus were so important. It was only after Columbus had discovered our country that other explorers and settlers from Europe came to this land. The story of our country really begins with the story of Christopher Columbus.

6. CHRISTOPHER COLUMBUS DISCOVERS AMERICA

STUDY LESSON

WHO AM I? Write the name of each of the following persons. Next to it, write the sentence which tells you about the person.

1. Columbus
2. Diego
3. Marco Polo
4. Isabella
5. Vasco da Gama
6. Juan Perez

a. I helped Columbus.
b. I was the first to sail around Africa to India.
c. I blessed the ships of Columbus before they left Spain.
d. I was the son of Columbus.
e. I discovered the New World.
f. Columbus read my book about the Far East.

SOMETHING TO THINK ABOUT. Think carefully before answering these questions.

1. Why did Columbus want to sail west?
2. At first, why wouldn't the Spaniards help Columbus?
3. Why did his people think that Vasco da Gama was a greater hero than Columbus?
4. Why was Columbus surprised not to find any cities in the New World?
5. Why was Columbus' first voyage very difficult?
6. Why was the discovery of Columbus more important than that of Leif Ericson?
7. Why do we know that the Faith of Columbus was strong?

WHAT AM I? Write each word and after it the phrase that explains it.

1. Moors
2. Indians
3. Holy Communion
4. Santa Maria
5. New World

a. lands discovered by Columbus.
b. people whom the Spanish were fighting in 1492.
c. the largest of Columbus' ships.
d. name Columbus gave the people he found in the New World.
e. spiritual help which Columbus and his men received before sailing.

DATES TO REMEMBER. Write the dates in column A. Next to each date write the sentence in column B that matches it.

A	B
1. 1446	a. The Portuguese reached India
2. 1492	b. Columbus died.
3. 1498	c. Columbus reached the New World.
4. 1506	d. Columbus was born about this time.

WORDS TO KNOW. Use each of these words in a sentence. Use your dictionary if you do not know their meaning.

**printing   monastery   jewels
fleet   harbor   hymn**

7. People in Europe Learn About America

John Cabot Discovers North America. These men have just landed on the coast of North America. Their leader is John Cabot. It is the year 1497. They are the first people from Europe who have seen North America since the visits of the Northmen.

The men have put up a cross. Now they are putting up the flag of England. This means that the land belongs to England.

John Cabot was born in Genoa. Columbus was born in this same city. Cabot was born about the same time as Columbus. He had the same idea that Columbus had — he said a ship should be able to reach the Far East by sailing to the west. The king of England paid for Cabot's voyage. John Cabot sailed farther north than Columbus. He landed on the coast of North America. Columbus had

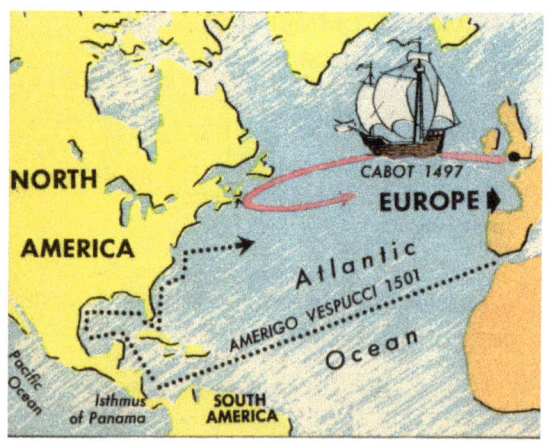

7. People in Europe Learn About America

seen South America, but he had not seen North America.

John Cabot, however, did not know he was in North America. Like Columbus he thought he had reached the Far East.

John Cabot's voyage was very important. Years later the English people said that North America belonged to them. They said it belonged to them because John Cabot was sailing for the King of England when he discovered North America.

How America Was Named. After Columbus made his first voyage, many men from Europe sailed to America. John Cabot was one of these men. Amerigo Vespucci was another. North America and South America are named after Amerigo Vespucci.

"How did this happen?" you ask. "Why weren't these lands named after Columbus?"

This is what happened: Amerigo Vespucci made a voyage to South America in 1501. When he came home he wrote the story of his trip. A man in Germany was writing a geography. He read what Amerigo Vespucci had written and made a map of the lands Amerigo Vespucci had visited. He thought Vespucci had discovered the land. He said the land should be named after Vespucci. So he wrote the word "America" on the map. He got this from Vespucci's first name.

Later, it was found that there were two continents in the New World. The name America was given to both of them. So we have North America and South America.

THE GREAT MISTAKE
America Is Named After Wrong Man

Aren't you glad the German map maker used Amerigo Vespucci's first name and not his last name?

Balboa Discovers the Pacific Ocean. Columbus had claimed the New World for Spain. Soon after his discovery, many Spaniards came to the New World. Some started farms on the islands near North America. Others searched for gold. These Spaniards thought they were in the Far East. They did not know that the Far East was really thousands of miles away. They were puzzled because they could not find the land of the Great Khan.

Vasco de Balboa was one of the Spaniards who came to the New World. One day an old Indian told Balboa that in the south there was a land that had much gold. Balboa took a group of men and started out to find this land. They crossed the Isthmus of Panama in 1513.

One day Balboa climbed to the top of a high hill. In the distance he saw water. He was puzzled.

What water was this? It looked like a great ocean, but the Atlantic Ocean was in the other direction. Balboa and his men marched on until they reached the water. It was an ocean all right. Balboa made a wooden cross. He waded into the water with it. Then he said that the ocean and all the land washed by it belonged to the King of Spain.

Balboa had discovered the Pacific Ocean.

The people of Europe heard about Balboa's discovery. They said: "This probably means that the lands which Columbus discovered are not in the Far East after all. This ocean probably lies between the new lands and the Far East."

For the first time, the people of Europe were learning that Columbus had not reached the Far East. He had discovered a New World.

Magellan's Ship Sails Around the World. Ferdinand Magellan was a sea captain who had been born in Portugal. He was very much interested when he learned that Balboa had discovered an ocean west of America.

7. People in Europe Learn About America

"Now we know that there is an ocean on the other side of America," he thought. "Suppose I could find a way to sail around America, or through America. Then my ships would be on the ocean Balboa discovered. Then I should be able to sail on to the Far East. I would do what Columbus tried to do. I would reach the Far East by sailing west."

The King of Spain helped Magellan. In August, 1519, Magellan left Spain with five ships. They sailed to the coast of South America. He sailed down the coast for many weeks. He could not find a way to sail around the continent. His men became frightened. They begged Magellan to turn back. He would not do so.

At last, they came to the southern end of South America. Here they found a narrow strip of water. Today, this strip of water is called the Strait of Magellan. They sailed through this strait. Then they were on the Pacific Ocean. Only two of the five ships were left by this time.

The two ships started across the Pacific Ocean. Magellan did not know what a big ocean this was. It took him three months to cross the ocean. The men ran out of food, and some of them starved to death.

At last Magellan reached a group of islands. He named them the Philippines in honor of King Philip of Spain. The Philippines are in the Far East. Magellan had proved that Columbus was right. He had reached the Far East by sailing west.

Magellan was killed in the Philippines. One of his ships, the *Victoria*, continued the voyage. It sailed the rest of the way

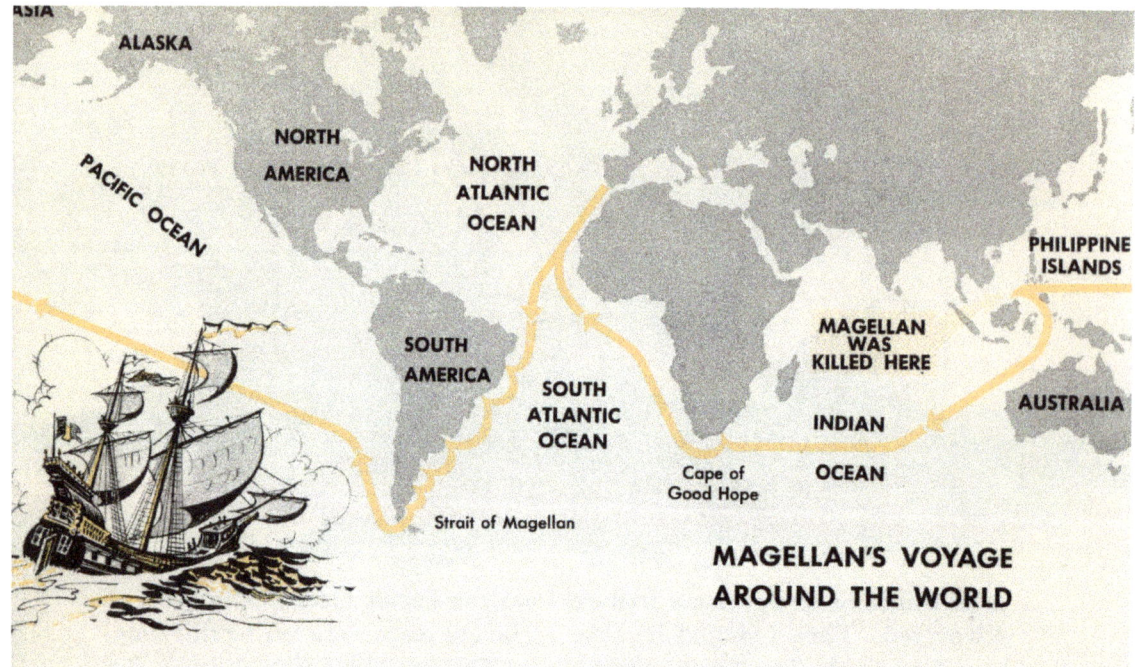

MAGELLAN'S VOYAGE AROUND THE WORLD

around the world and reached Spain in 1522. This was the first ship to sail around the world.

This voyage proved three things: It proved that the world was much larger than anyone had thought. 2. It proved that the Pacific was the world's largest ocean. 3. It proved that America was thousands of miles from the Far East.

There were only thirty years between the time Columbus made his first voyage and the time the Victoria returned to Spain. In that time, the people of Europe had learned much about the world. They had discovered the great continents of North America and South America, and the Pacific Ocean which covers half the world.

The people of Europe still wanted to reach the Far East. But now they knew that they had to go around or get through America, before they could reach the Far East.

STUDY LESSON

WHO AM I? Write the name of each person listed. Next to it, write the sentence which tells you about the person.

1. Amerigo Vespucci
2. Ferdinand Magellan
3. John Cabot
4. Vasco de Balboa

a. I discovered North America for the English.
b. The New World was named after me.
c. I discovered the Pacific Ocean.
d. I was the captain of the first ship that sailed around the world.

WHAT AM I? Write each word and after it the phrase that explains it.

1. gold   2. strait   3. map maker
4. Victoria   5. North America

a. the job of the German who gave America its name.
b. what many Spaniards were looking for when they came to America.
c. the part of America Columbus never saw.
d. the waterway Magellan sailed through at the southern tip of South America.
e. the name of the first ship to sail around the world.

DATES TO REMEMBER. Write each date in column A. Next write the sentence in column B that matches the date.

A	B
1. 1497	a. Magellan's ship returns to Spain.
2. 1522	b. The Pacific Ocean is discovered.
3. 1513	c. John Cabot lands in North America.

WHERE AM I? Write the name of each place, and next to it, the sentence which tells where it is.

1. Spain   2. Strait of Magellan
3. Isthmus of Panama   4. Philippines

a. The first ship to sail around the world sailed from this country.
b. Magellan lost his life in these islands.
c. It connects the Atlantic and Pacific oceans.
d. Balboa crossed this narrow strip of land.

SOMETHING TO THINK ABOUT. Think carefully before you answer these questions.

1. Why did the English lay claim to North America?
2. Why did Magellan not finish his voyage around the world?
3. How did Balboa know that he was not in the Far East?
4. Why was the New World not named after Columbus?
5. Why was the voyage of Magellan important to the people of Europe?

WORDS TO KNOW. Use each of the following words in a sentence. Look them up in a dictionary if you are not sure of the meaning.

island   isthmus   geography

GAMES

SCRAPBOOK OF FAMOUS PEOPLE

THROUGH THE PAGES OF THIS BOOK YOU WILL LEARN ABOUT MANY FAMOUS MEN IN HISTORY. START NOW TO WRITE YOUR OWN STORIES ABOUT THEM AND MAKE A "SCRAPBOOK OF FAMOUS PEOPLE." PUT IN IT SOME OF THE GREAT MEN AND WOMEN YOU WILL MEET AS YOU STUDY HISTORY. AFTER YOU WRITE A STORY ABOUT ONE OF YOUR FAVORITES, TRY TO FIND HIS OR HER PICTURE OR DRAW ONE TO GO WITH YOUR STORY. HERE ARE TWO NAMES TO START YOUR SCRAPBOOK!

COLUMBUS • MAGELLAN

WORKING TOGETHER

YOU MIGHT WRITE A FEW PARAGRAPHS ABOUT THE DARING OF COLUMBUS AND THE BRAVERY OF MAGELLAN.

SEVERAL BOYS AND GIRLS IN THE CLASS CAN WORK TOGETHER ON THIS PROJECT. MAKE A SET OF POSTERS SHOWING COLUMBUS'S FIRST TRIP TO THE NEW WORLD. YOU MIGHT DRAW THESE SCENES:

1. THE THREE SHIPS IN HARBOR AT PALOS
2. FATHER PEREZ GIVING HIS BLESSING
3. THE THREE SHIPS IN A STORM AT SEA
4. THE SHIPS AT PORT IN THE HARBOR OF SAN SALVADOR WITH SOME INDIANS ON THE SHORE

BOAT BUILDER

MAKE A MODEL OF A NORSE SHIP. YOU MIGHT USE CARDBOARD OR BALSA WOOD, MODELLING CLAY, OR EVEN SOAP. BE SURE YOUR MODEL SHOWS:

1. A CARVED OR PAINTED DRAGON ON THE PROW
2. A BLACK HULL
3. A TALL SQUARE SAIL

7. People in Europe Learn About America

ART · BOOKS · PLAYS

NAME GAME

DIVIDE THE CLASS INTO TWO SIDES. LET ONE PUPIL GIVE TWO CLUES ABOUT A PERSON WHO HAS APPEARED IN THIS UNIT, SUCH AS, "HE WAS A NORSEMAN. HIS FATHER WAS KNOWN AS ERIC, THE RED." THE FIRST CHILD ON THE OTHER SIDE MUST BE ABLE TO SOLVE THE MYSTERY NAME FROM THE CLUES GIVEN. IF HE DOES NOT GIVE THE CORRECT ANSWER, "LEIF ERICSON," HE IS DROPPED FROM THE TEAM. WHEN THERE ARE NO MEMBERS LEFT ON ONE TEAM, THE OTHER TEAM IS THE WINNER.

THIS IS HOW IT HAPPENED

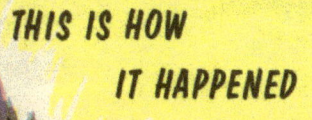

PLAN A PLAY CALLED "BEYOND THE AZORES."

SCENE I: COLUMBUS VISITS FERDINAND AND ISABELLA
SCENE II: COLUMBUS MEETS FATHER PEREZ
SCENE III: COLUMBUS AGAIN VISITS FERDINAND AND ISABELLA
SCENE IV: COLUMBUS SAILS FROM SPAIN ON HIS VOYAGE
SCENE V: COLUMBUS, WHILE WORRYING ABOUT A MUTINY, DISCOVERS LAND

INDIAN INFORMATION POST

WOULD YOU LIKE TO KNOW MORE ABOUT INDIANS—THE FIRST AMERICANS? THERE ARE MANY DIFFERENT TRIBES OF INDIANS AND THERE ARE MANY DIFFERENT BOOKS ABOUT THEM. IF YOU WOULD LIKE TO LEARN ABOUT THE INDIANS FIND ONE OF THESE BOOKS IN A LIBRARY. THERE ARE ALSO SOME BOOKS ABOUT OTHER PEOPLE WHOM YOU HAVE READ ABOUT.

Author	Title	Publisher
ABEITA	I AM A PUEBLO INDIAN GIRL	MORROW
BLEEKER	INDIANS OF THE LONGHOUSE	MORROW
BRINDZE	THE STORY OF THE TOTEM POLE	VANGUARD
DEMING	INDIANS OF THE WIGWAMS	WHITMAN
HOLLING	BOOK OF INDIANS	PLATT
AULAIRE	LEIF THE LUCKY	DOUBLEDAY
DUVOISIN	THEY PUT OUT TO SEA	KNOPF
GRAHAM	CHRISTOPHER COLUMBUS, DISCOVERER	ABINGTON-COKESBURY

Looking Into the Long Ago

Mary Jean could hardly believe her eyes when she stepped from the car.

Some friends were going for a drive and had offered to take her to her uncle's farm. Mary knew that her cousin Dick would be waiting for her at the end of the lane. But she had not expected him to be dressed like this. And those boys with him! They were also dressed in costumes of some kind.

"Hello, Mary Jean," cried Dick. "Welcome to the North farm." Turning to the other boys he said: "You remember my friends Bill and Pete and Louis."

"Hello, boys," said Mary Jean. "Why in the world are you wearing those costumes?"

Dick winked at his friends. Mary Jean did not see the wink.

"What costumes?" he asked. "You know what costumes!" "You mean these clothes!" said Dick. He sounded surprised.

"All right," Mary Jean said as they started walking down the lane. "If you won't tell me, I'll ask your mother and father."

Mr. and Mrs. North were waiting at the front door of the farm house. After Mary Jean greeted them, she said: "Uncle Tom and Aunt Martha, why are the boys dressed in those costumes?"

Mr. North laughed. "You came at just the right time, Mary Jean.

"They are going to be in a history program at their school. Each boy is dressed like a man from a different part of Europe. These are some of the men who came to America from Europe."

"So that's it!" cried Mary Jean.

"Tell her what you are, Pete," said Mr. North.

"I'm a Spanish soldier," said Pete.

"The Spaniards were the first people from Europe to come to America," said Mr. North. "Soon, they ruled a large part of North America and South America. They ruled about one-third of the land that is now the United States. Pete here is dressed like a soldier, but many men besides soldiers came from Spain. Many priests came. They told the Indians about the One True Church. Because of these priests, many Indians became Catholics."

"And who are you, Louis?" Mary Jean asked.

"I'm a French fur trader."

"The French once ruled a large part of Canada," said Mr. North. "They also ruled a large part of what is now the United States. Many French fur traders traveled through the forests. They bought furs from the Indians. But not all the French were fur traders. There were farmers, too. And many priests came from France."

"I'm a Dutch settler," said Bill. "I came from Holland and lived in New Amsterdam. That is New York City now."

"Yes," said Mr. North, "the Dutch were the first to settle in New York City and New York State."

"And, my dear cousin," said Dick, "I am from England. I am one of the first settlers at Jamestown, Virginia."

"Really?" said Mary Jean. There was a twinkle in her eyes. "I did not know you were quite that old."

"Now you boys run along," said Mrs. North.

"Well, they really had me puzzled," laughed Mary Jean. "That's interesting about the Spaniards, the French, the Dutch, and the English.

"You will learn more about them soon," said Mr. North. "If I am not mistaken, the next part of your history will be about them. But I know you are anxious to see your pet calf, Goldie. She has grown up so much you will hardly know her."

"Oh, I can't wait to see her," said Mary Jean. As she started to run off, she said, "Tell your son, the Jamestown settler, that I'll be down in the barnyard with Goldie."

8. The Spaniards Settle in the South

Cortez Find a Great City. The men in this picture are Spanish soldiers. They are in Mexico. It is the year 1519. The leader of the soldiers is a man named Hernando Cortez.

Cortez and his men have marched many miles across Mexico. Now they have come to a large city. They are amazed because they have never before seen anything like this in the New World. The city belongs to the Aztec Indians.

The city is on the an island in the lake. Roads go across the lake to the city. The city has many big buildings.

In Chapter 1 we read about the Indians who lived in the United States before the white men came. We read that these Indians had no big cities. But the Aztecs were not in the United States. They were in Mexico.

Cortez Conquers the Aztecs. The king of the Aztecs came out of the city to meet Cortez. The king's name was Montezuma. Montezuma was carried

8. The Spaniards Settle in the South

in a litter on the shoulders of his men. He wore a cloak trimmed with gold and jewels. The other Aztecs kept their eyes on the ground. They were not allowed to look at their ruler. Montezuma invited Cortez and his men to stay at his palace.

Montezuma ruled a large part of Mexico. The Aztecs had conquered all the other tribes in that part of the country.

The Spanish soldiers were amazed when they saw the grand palace where Montezuma lived. They were also amazed at other sights in the city. They saw that the Aztecs had great treasures of gold, silver, pearls, and precious stones.

The Spaniards also saw something they did not like. The Aztecs had many false gods. They thought they could please their gods by killing people. The Aztecs captured people from other tribes. These people were taken to the temples and killed. Hundreds and hundreds of people were killed in this way.

After a while fighting broke out between the Spaniards and the Aztecs. Most of the Spaniards were killed. Cortez escaped from the city with a few of his men.

Then Cortez asked the other Indian tribes to help him. Most of them were glad to do so. They did not like the way Montezuma ruled them. Cortez surrounded the city of the Aztecs. The Aztecs were forced to surrender.

Cortez now said that Mexico belonged to Spain.

Cortez tore down the temples to the false gods. He sent for Catholic priests. These priests built churches where the temples had been. They taught the Indians about God. Many Indians became Catholics.

The city of the Aztecs was given a new name. It was called Mexico City. The governor of all the Spanish lands in the New World went to live in Mexico City.

The Blessed Virgin Appears to an Indian. A wonderful thing happened near Mexico City in 1531. This was just ten years after Cortez conquered the city.

Juan Diego was a poor Aztec Indian who had become a Catholic. He lived near Mexico City. One Saturday morning he was on his way to Mass. As he climbed a small hill, he saw a beautiful lady. Her dress was shining bright like the sun.

The Lady said: "I am holy Mary, ever Virgin Mother of the true God." She asked Juan to tell the Bishop that she wished a church built at that spot.

Juan went to the Bishop, but the Bishop did not know what to do. How could he be sure that Our Lady had appeared to Juan? He thought Juan might have imagined it. The Blessed Mother appeared a second time. Again she asked

8. The Spaniards Settle in the South

When the Bishop opened the cloak the roses fell to the floor. But the Bishop saw something more marvelous than the roses. On the cloak there was a beautiful picture of the Blessed Virgin. The Bishop and all the others who were in the room fell to their knees. The Blessed Virgin left her picture on the cloak so that the Bishop would know that she had really appeared.

Indians in many parts of the New World heard that Mary had appeared to Juan Diego. They came from many miles away to pray in the church that was built in Mary's honor. Many more Indians became Catholics. About eight million Indians became Catholics in the next ten years.

When Mary appeared in Mexico she asked to be called Our Lady of Guadalupe. Today there is still a great shrine to Our Lady of Guadalupe. Thousands of people visit this shrine every year. December 12th is the feast of Our Lady of Guadalupe. This is a national holiday in Mexico.

Our Lady of Guadalupe belongs not only to Mexico but to all the New World. In 1945 Pope Pius XII called her the Empress of America.

Pizarro Conquers Peru. After Cortez conquered Mexico, many other Spaniards went to other parts of the New World.

for a church. Again the Bishop did not know what to do.

The third time the Blessed Mother told Juan to go to a bush that was close by and pick some roses. Juan obeyed. This was a wonderful thing because it was December. Roses do not usually bloom in Mexico in December. The Blessed Mother put the roses in Juan's cloak. She told Juan to take the roses to the Bishop.

8. The Spaniards Settle in the South

Francisco Pizarro went to Peru. Peru is in South America. Find it on the map. In Peru, Pizarro conquered the Incas. The Incas were as wealthy as the Aztecs. Both Cortez and Pizarro sent much treasure back to Spain. Spain became the richest country in the world.

Pizarro said that Peru belonged to the King of Spain. Other Spaniards claimed other parts of South America for Spain. Soon, the King of Spain ruled a large part of that continent. Many Spaniards moved to South America.

Spaniards in the United States. Other Spaniards visited the land that is now the United States.

Hernando de Soto explored the land near the Gulf of Mexico. In 1541 his men discovered the Mississippi River. This is the largest river in the United

Indian Guide and DeSoto in Sight of Mississippi

States. De Soto and his men crossed the Mississippi near the place where it empties into the Gulf of Mexico.

Francisco Coronado led an army through what are now the states of Arizona, New Mexico, Texas, Oklahoma, and Kansas. He was searching for the "Seven Cities of Cibola." He had heard that these cities were so rich that the roofs of the houses were covered with gold. Instead he found nothing but clay houses called pueblos. The Indians who lived in them were poor and had no gold. Because of De Soto and Coronado, the Spaniards claimed almost all the southern part of our country.

Ponce de Leon discovered Florida in 1513. Twice he failed to make a lasting colony. Later on, in 1565 some Spaniards built a fort on the coast of Florida. They named it St. Augustine. It is the oldest city in the United States.

The most important cities started by the Spanish were Mexico City in Mexico and Lima in Peru. The Spaniards also started some of the other cities of the United States. Los Angeles and San Francisco are two of the biggest.

The Spaniards Brought the True Faith to the New World. Many priests from Spain came to the New World. They came to teach the Indians about the true Church.

In some parts of the New World the Indians were very unfriendly. They killed the Spanish priests. When a person is

killed for his faith, we call him a martyr. Many of the Spanish priests were martyrs.

They brought down great blessings on the Church in the New World.

In the southwest the Indians were friendlier. Here the Spanish priests built missions.

Each mission had many buildings. The most important building was the church. Usually there was a picture or a statue of Our Lady of Guadalupe somewhere in the church. Each mission had a school, a workshop, a home for the priests, and homes for the Indians. Each mission had a large farm. The priests at the mission taught the Indians to read and write. They taught them to be better farmers. Some learned how to be carpenters. Others learned to make soap, candles, and blankets. The missionaries helped to keep the Indians from being slaves of Spanish rulers. The most important thing the priests taught the Indians was the Catholic religion.

Father Junipero Serra was one of the most famous Spanish priests in the New World. Father Serra belonged to the Franciscan Order. He built nine missions in California. After he died other Franciscans built other missions.

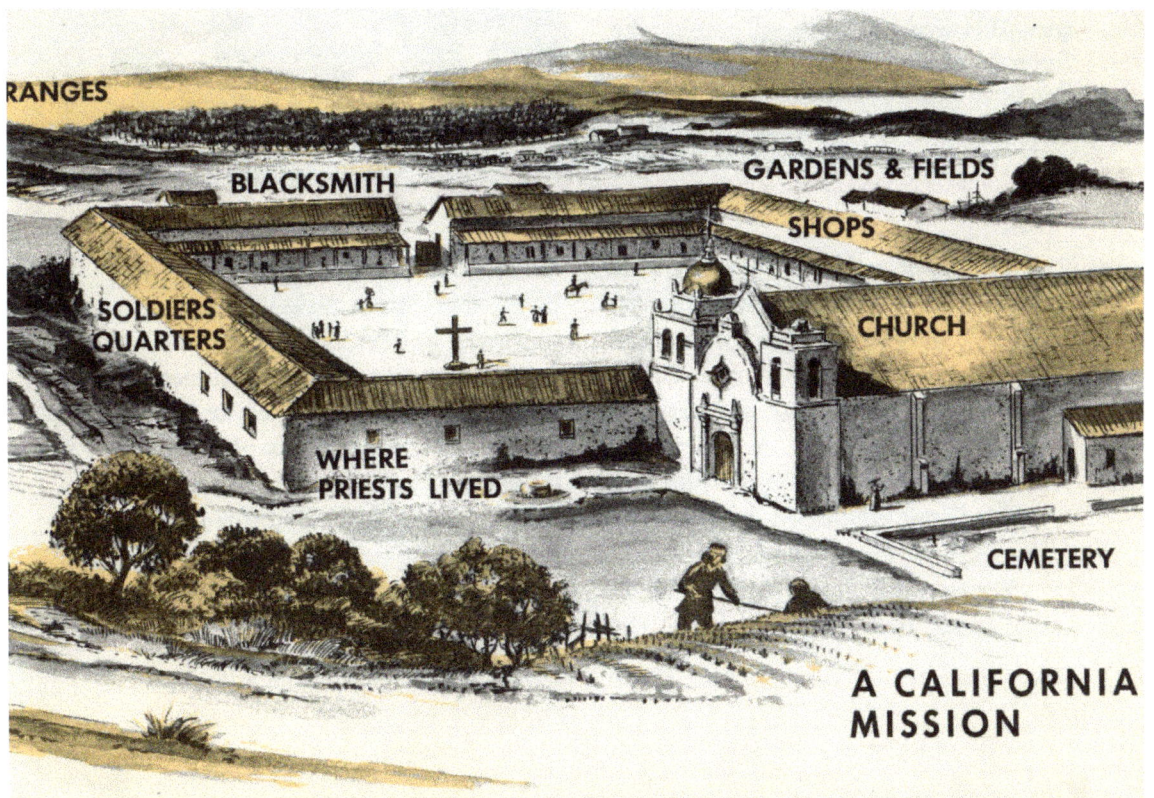

A CALIFORNIA MISSION

Finally, there were 21 of these missions in California. Some of the California missions are still standing.

The Spaniards Ruled a Big Part of the New World. The map on page 60 shows that Spain once ruled a big part of the New World. Spain ruled much of South America. She ruled all of Central America and Mexico, and many islands. She also ruled about one-third of the land that is now the United States.

There were fewer Spaniards in the land that later became the United States than in the other lands that Spain ruled.

Today in Mexico, Central America, and most of the countries of South America the people speak Spanish. Most of the people in these lands are Catholics. This reminds us that Spain once ruled these lands. It also reminds us that Spain brought a great gift to these lands. That gift was the Catholic religion.

8. The Spaniards Settle in the South

STUDY LESSON

WHO AM I? Write the name of each person listed. Next to it, write the sentence which tells you about the person.

1. Junipero Serra
2. Hernando de Soto
3. Juan Diego
4. Hernando Cortez
5. Francisco Pizarro
6. Montezuma

a. I conquered the Aztecs of Mexico.
b. The Blessed Virgin appeared to me at Guadalupe.
c. I conquered the Incas of Peru.
d. I am the ruler of the rich Aztec Indians.
e. I found the largest river in the United States.
f. I am a Spanish priest who built missions in California.

WHAT AM I? Write each word and after it the phrase that explains it.

1. martyr 2. mission
3. Saint Augustine

a. a church and other buildings in which Indians were taught.
b. the oldest city in the United States.
c. a person killed for his faith.

WHERE IS IT? Write the name of each place, and next to it, the phrase which tells where it is or what it is.

1. Los Angeles 2. Lima 3. Mississippi

a. the longest river in the United States.
b. a city in California started by the Spanish.
c. an old city in the land of the Incas.

DATES TO REMEMBER. Write each date in column A. Next to it write the sentence in column B that matches the date.

A	B
1. 1541	a. the beginning of the city of Saint Augustine.
2. 1565	b. the finding of the Mississippi River.

SOMETHING TO THINK ABOUT. Think carefully before you answer these questions.

1. Why were the Indians treated well under the Spaniards?
2. Why did Our Lady appear to Juan Diego?
3. Why are there so many Catholic names in California? Name some.

WORDS TO KNOW. Write a sentence using each of these words.

**palace   cloak   ruler
garment   marvelous   Empress**

9. The English Settle at Jamestown

How Jamestown Was Founded. The people of England heard many stories about America. They heard that the Spaniards were bringing shiploads of gold from Mexico and Peru. The English thought that they too should have some of the wealth of the New World.

"After all, North America belongs to us," many Englishmen thought. "John Cabot discovered the continent in 1497. He claimed it for the King of England."

Several groups of Englishmen came to North America to start settlements. But they found life very hard in the American wilderness. After a short time these settlers gave up. They left North America and went back to England.

Then some London merchants organized a company called the London

9. The English Settle at Jamestown

In the picture, we see the men landing. This happened on May 14, 1607. This landing was an important event in the history of our country. These were the first English settlers who came to North America and stayed here. Years later, the English settlements were to become the United States of America.

The settlement which was built in Virginia was called Jamestown. The river was called the James. Both the town and the river were named for King James I of England.

Captain John Smith Saves Jamestown. Many of these first settlers did not want to work very hard. They should have been building houses and a fort. They should have been planting crops. Instead, they spent much of their time hunting for gold. When winter came they had very little food. It looked as if they would either die of the cold or starve to death.

Then Captain John Smith was put in charge of the settlement. Captain John Smith saved the settlement. He made the men work. "If you do not work, you shall not eat," he said. So the men finished the fort. They built better houses to protect themselves from the winter weather. Captain Smith also traded with the Indians. He gave the Indians beads and hatchets. In return, they gave him food.

Company. The London Company sent a group of men to start a settlement in North America. The men left England in December, 1606. It took the ships four months to cross the Atlantic Ocean. In April, 1607 they reached the part of North America that was named Virginia. The ships sailed about Chesapeake Bay for a time. The men found a river which emptied into the bay. They sailed up the river. There they found a place where they thought they would like to build their settlement.

In this way, John Smith kept the settlers from starving to death.

How John Smith's Life Was Saved. Soon after the settlers landed John Smith had an exciting adventure. He was captured by Indians. The Indians were going to shoot him with their arrows. Then he pulled a compass out of his pocket. The Indians had never seen anything like it before. They gathered around to look at the compass. They decided to take John Smith to their chief.

The name of the chief was Powhatan. Powhatan talked for a long time with the other leaders of the tribe. They decided that John Smith should be put to death. His hands and feet were tied. His head was put on a big stone. Two Indian warriors stood over him with clubs. They were ready to strike.

Suddenly Powhatan's little daughter ran out and put her arms around John Smith's neck. The girl's name was Pocahontas. The warriors could not hit Smith without hitting Pocahontas. The girl begged Powhatan to spare Smith's life. Powhatan loved his daughter and did as she asked. Smith was set free.

After that John Smith and Powhatan became friends. That is why the Indians sold food to Smith.

John Smith Returns to England. After he was at Jamestown two years John Smith was hurt when some gunpowder exploded. He had to go back to England to have the wounds treated. He never returned to Jamestown. He explored the coast of southern Canada and northern United States. He wrote about America

9. The English Settle at Jamestown

and encouraged many more English settlers to go there.

One day in 1616 John Smith heard that an old friend of his was in London. It was Pocahontas. She had married a settler named John Rolfe. She and her husband had come to London for a visit. John Smith went to visit her. She was dressed in fine clothes and looked very beautiful. While she was in London she visited the Queen.

All of a sudden Pocahontas became sick. She died before she could go back to America with her husband and baby son.

Jamestown Grows Into Virginia Colony. There were about five hundred men at Jamestown when John Smith went back to England.

These men did not have another good leader to take Smith's place. The men went back to their lazy ways. They did not have enough to eat. The Indians became unfriendly and would not sell them food. During the winter most of the settlers died. That winter was called the "Starving Time."

Only sixty settlers were left when spring came. These sixty men got on a ship to sail back to England. As they were going down the river they met three ships coming from England. These ships were loaded with food and with men who knew how to work. The sixty settlers turned around and went back to Jamestown. The English were in America to stay.

How Our Nation Began

The English settlers never did find any gold near Jamestown. But they learned to raise tobacco, and tobacco sold for good prices in England. Soon there were many other settlements near Jamestown. The settlements grew into the colony of Virginia.

What do we mean when we say that Virginia was a colony? We mean that Virginia was not a free country. Virginia was owned and ruled by England. Therefore, Virginia was said to be a colony of England.

Before long England started other colonies besides Virginia. We shall read about these colonies later in the book.

Spain, France, Holland, and Sweden also had colonies in North America.

1619 Was an Important Year. Three important things happened in Virginia in 1619.

9. The English Settle at Jamestown

In that year women arrived in Virginia to become the wives of the settlers. Until this time, only men had lived in Virginia. Now there would be families. A ship also arrived bringing some Negroes. They were stolen from their homes in Africa and sold to the settlers as slaves.

The slaves had to do exactly what their owners told them. They were not paid for their work. Most of them were put to work in the tobacco fields. The owners could sell their slaves to other settlers, just as they would sell horses or cattle. We know that this was wrong. Human beings have souls made in the image and likeness of God. It is wrong to treat them like animals. Slavery caused much trouble in our country.

The First Assembly. We have read about two of the important things that happened in 1619. What was the third thing?

In that year the Virginia assembly met for the first time. The members of this assembly had been elected by the people. They were to make laws for Virginia.

Virginia was still a colony of England. But England was far away from Virginia. The men who were the leaders in England did not know very much about Virginia. They did not make many laws for Virginia. The assembly was allowed to make most of the laws for the well being of the colonists.

When other English colonies were started they also had assemblies. The English colonists were proud of their assemblies. In most of the countries of Europe at that time the people were ruled by kings. They had to do what their king told them to do. If the king was good, the people were treated kindly. If he was bad the people suffered.

"But our laws are made in our assemblies," said the colonists. "We elect the members of the assemblies, so they try to do what we wish. We really rule ourselves."

This was true as long as the government in England was not strict with the colonies.

9. THE ENGLISH SETTLE AT JAMESTOWN

STUDY LESSON

WHO AM I? Write the names of each person listed. Next to it write the sentence which tells you about the person.

1. Powhatan   2. John Smith
3. John Rolfe   4. Pocahontas
5. John Cabot

a. I am the leader of the English colony at Jamestown.
b. I am an Indian chieftain.
c. I claimed North America for the King of England.
d. I saved the life of John Smith.
e. I married the Indian princess, Pocahontas.

SOMETHING TO THINK ABOUT. Think carefully before you answer these questions.

1. Why do you think Pocahontas saved John Smith?
2. Why did Powhatan listen to Pocahontas?
3. Why did the settlers not want to do any work?
4. What did John Smith say to make the settlers work?
5. Do you think that John Smith was right?
6. Why is slavery wrong?
7. Why was the year 1619 a good year for the English colonists?

WHAT AM I? Write each word and after it the phrase that explains it.

1. Jamestown   2. Virginia   3. tobacco

a. the crop the settlers learned to raise.
b. the first permanent English settlement in the New World.
c. the colony that grew up around the first English settlement.

DATES TO REMEMBER. Write each date in column A. Next to it write the phrase in column B that matches the date.

A	B
1. 1497	a. the first settlement in the New World by the English.
2. 1619	b. the first meeting of the Virginia Assembly.
3. 1607	c. the first English discovery in the New World.

WORDS TO KNOW. Write a sentence using each of these words. Look them up in your dictionary if you are not sure of the meaning.

compass   **wilderness**   **warrior**
assembly   **colony**   **slave**

10. The French Settle in the North

French Fishermen Come to the New World. The first Frenchmen who came to the New World were fishermen. Every year a number of fishing ships left the port of St. Malo in France. They sailed across the Atlantic Ocean to Newfoundland. The wives and mothers of the fishermen dreaded to see them go. It would be months before they returned to France. Always there were some men who did not return, because it was a dangerous voyage.

There are many fish in the water near Newfoundland. That is why the French fishermen sailed so many miles to get there. In the picture above we see some of these fishermen. They are pulling in a net full of fish. Later they will take the fish to the coast of Newfoundland. There they will dry the fish and store them until they are ready to sail back to France.

John Verrazano Explores the Coast. The fishermen did not learn very much about North America. They were interested only in catching fish and then returning to France.

King Francis I of France wished to learn more about North America. He also wished to learn if a ship could get through North America and then sail on to the Far East.

King Francis hired an Italian sea captain named John Verrazano. He asked Verrazano to find out more about North America. Verrazano's ship reached North America in 1524. He traveled from North Carolina to Newfoundland. He made many maps. He sailed into New York harbor. His men were probably the first white men to see this great harbor.

Verrazano saw many parts of North America that no one from Europe had ever seen before. For this reason, the French later said that much of North America belonged to them.

10. The French Settle in the North

Cartier Finds the St. Lawrence. Ten years later King Francis sent another man to find a passage through North America. This man was Jacques Cartier, a Catholic from St. Malo, France. On August 10, the feast of St. Lawrence, Cartier discovered a large body of water. He named it the Gulf of St. Lawrence to honor the saint of the day. The river which emptied into the gulf was named the St. Lawrence River. Cartier put up a great wooden cross. On the cross were the words "Long Live the King of France."

The next year Cartier came back to North America. He sailed up the St. Lawrence River. He hoped this river would lead to the Pacific Ocean. He came to rapids and could not sail any farther. Cartier visited an island in the river. There was an Indian village on the island. Behind the village there was a high hill. The view from the top of this hill was so beautiful that Cartier named it Montreal,

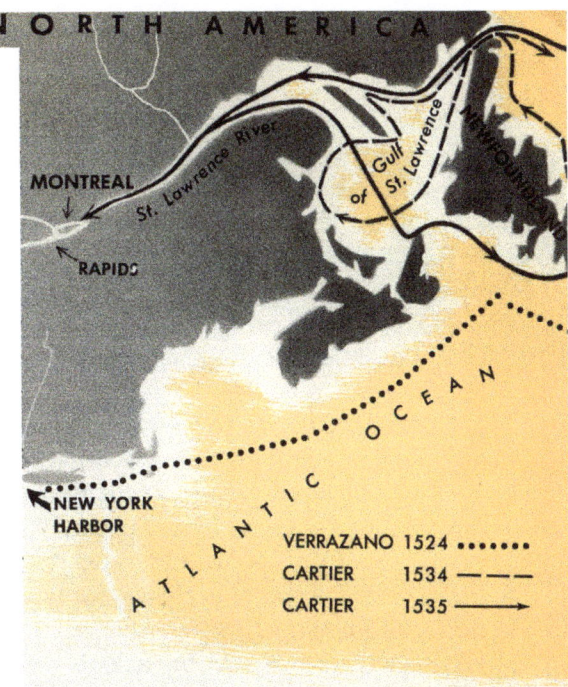

meaning Mount Royal. Today, the great city of Montreal is at the foot of this hill.

Cartier made four voyages to America. On one of his voyages he tried to start a settlement. But the winter was too cold and the men returned to France.

The "Father of New France." The work which was begun by Cartier was carried on by Samuel de Champlain. Champlain first came to North America in 1603. In 1608 he started a tiny fort and settlement at Quebec. This was just one year after the English had started a settlement at Jamestown.

Quebec became an important fur trading post. Indians trapped animals in the forest. They brought the furs to Quebec. The French gave the Indians beads and other goods from Europe in exchange for the furs. Then the furs were sent to France where they sold for a high price.

Champlain made friends with the Huron Indians and the Algonquin Indians. He brought priests from France to teach the Indians about the Catholic religion.

The Iroquois Indians lived in what is now New York State. They were enemies of the Algonquins. Champlain joined the Algonquins in the war against the Iroquois. He marched many miles with the Algonquins. On the way he discovered a large lake. Today, we call it Lake Champlain. Can you find this lake on the map?

When it was time for the battle, Champlain put on his suit of armor. Then he marched out to meet the Iroquois. The Iroquois attacked. Champlain fired his gun. There was a loud noise and two of the Iroquois leaders dropped dead. The Iroquois were frightened. This was the first gun they had ever seen. They turned and fled. It was an easy victory for Champlain and

10. The French Settle in the North

the Algonquins. But after that the Iroquois were always bitter enemies of the French.

Later, Champlain discovered two of the Great Lakes: Lake Huron and Lake Ontario.

Champlain died in Quebec in 1635. This was 33 years after he had first come to the New World. He had started a rich fur trade for France, had founded several settlements, and had discovered a valuable chain of lakes and rivers. He is called the "Father of New France." New France was the name that was given to the settlements along the St. Lawrence River.

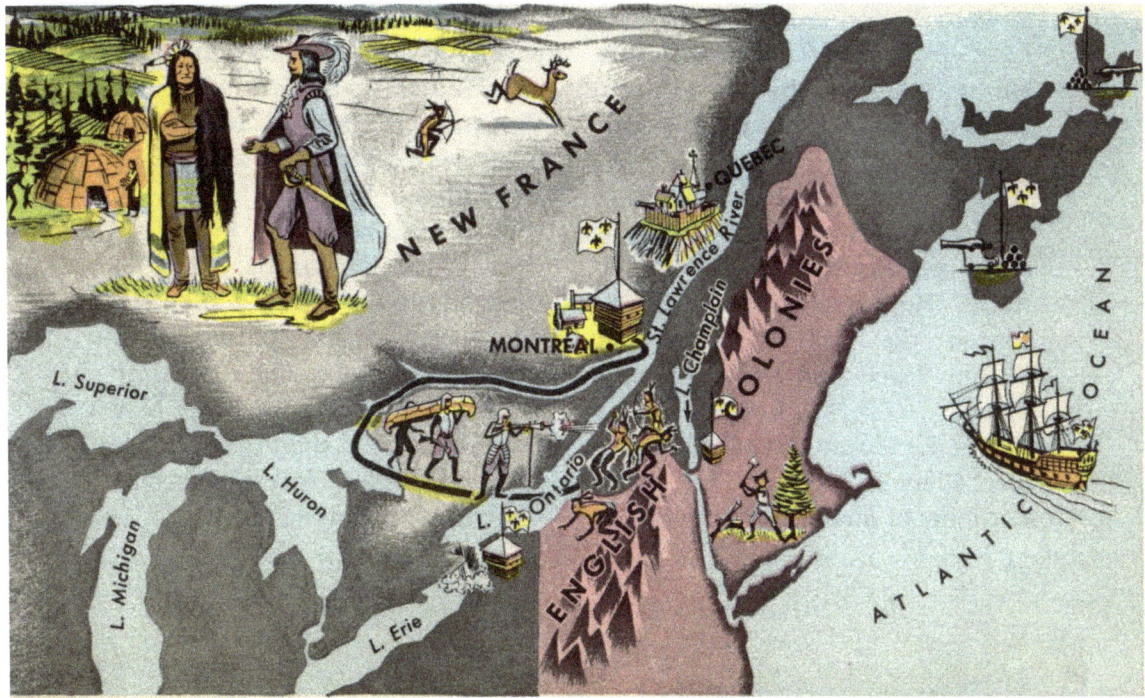

The North American Martyrs. The first priests who came to New France worked among the Huron Indians. The Hurons were friendly toward the French, and they were peace-loving people. In time, there were about 8,000 Catholic Hurons.

One of the French priests who came to North America was Father Isaac Jogues. He was a Jesuit. He wanted to help the peaceful Huron tribe. They were mostly farmers.

First Father Jogues had to learn the strange Huron language, so he could speak to them and be understood. He brought medicine and treated the sick Indians. The Hurons loved him and called him "Black Robe." Father Jogues taught the Hurons about Christ and His Blessed Mother. He made Catholics of almost the whole tribe.

Father Jogues worked among the Hurons for about six years. Then he wanted to teach other tribes about Our Lord. He went to visit the wild Iroquois. They quickly made him their prisoner. Father Jogues was tortured and his hands were mangled. He escaped and got to France. Then he begged his superiors to send him back to America. He and two companions visited the northern part of New York. They were captured by the Indians and killed.

About this same time, five Jesuits were killed in Canada. In 1930 these eight men were canonized. This means that the Church has declared them saints. The eight saints are called the North American Martyrs. A shrine in their memory is at Auriesville, New York. We should remember to pray to them.

A HOLY INDIAN GIRL

Catherine Tekakwitha was an Indian girl. She belonged to the Mohawk tribe. She is often called "The Lily of the Mohawks."

Catherine was born in 1656. She was born in a Mohawk village in what is now New York State. Father Jogues and his companions had been killed in this same village ten years before Catherine was born.

Catherine's father was a chief of the Mohawks. Her mother had belonged to another tribe of Indians. As a girl she met some priests and became a Catholic. Then Catherine's mother was captured by the Mohawks and carried away. This happened before Catherine was born.

Catherine was only four years old when her mother died. Then her father and her brother also died. Catherine was brought up by an uncle. Catherine was not baptized because no priest had come to the village. As a child she did not learn very much about the Catholic religion.

Three Jesuit priests came to the village when Catherine was ten years old. She loved to hear the priests talk about the One True God. She loved to hear the story of Our Lord. This was so different from the cruel religion of the Mohawks! In a few days the priests moved on to another village. But Catherine never forgot what they said.

Ten years passed. Another Jesuit priest came to the village. Catherine learned more about the Catholic religion from him. She was baptized on Easter Sunday in 1676. She was not quite twenty years old.

Catherine ran away from the Mohawk village. Her uncle started after her. He almost caught her, but she escaped. She went to a village of Christian Indians in Canada. There Catherine led a good and holy life. She died when she was twenty-four years old.

Today the Church allows us to call her Venerable Catherine Tekakwitha. This means that she is a Friend of God. Perhaps we may soon be allowed to call her Saint Catherine Tekakwitha.

Pray that this may come true.

Father Marquette Explores the Mississippi River. Another famous French missionary was Father Jacques Marquette. Father Marquette was also a Jesuit. While he was a young priest he was sent to Quebec. There he studied the customs of the Indians of Canada. Father Marquette learned a number of Indian languages so that he could preach to the Indians.

Father Marquette was very happy when at last he was sent on his first mission. This was on Lake Superior. Later he moved to a place near the Strait of Mackinac, which is between Lake Huron and Lake Michigan. A strait is a narrow body of water which connects two larger bodies of water.

Near the strait Father Marquette built a small chapel. The walls were made of bark from the trees. Father called his mission Saint Ignace. He began to teach the Indians about God and the Catholic religion. Father worked hard to help the Indians to live happier and better lives.

Some Indians told Father Marquette about a great river to the south. "Does this river flow into the Pacific Ocean?" wondered Father Marquette. "If so, this might be a way to reach the Far East."

10. The French Settle in the North

Father Marquette and a French fur trader named Louis Joliet set out to find this river. They had five other men with them. They were happy to have Father Marquette with them. Father knew how to speak the languages of the Indians. He understood their customs and loved them. Wherever he went Father won the respect of the Indians.

Father Marquette and his party paddled up the Fox River. Then they carried their canoes to the Wisconsin River. They floated down the Wisconsin River. At last their canoes floated out onto a great river. Father Marquette knew that this was the river he was looking for. He named it River of the Immaculate Conception. Today, we call it the Mississippi River. This was the name which the Indians gave the river, which they also called "Father of Waters."

This was the same river De Soto had discovered a hundred years earlier. But De Soto had seen only the part that is near the Gulf of Mexico. Father Marquette went down the river for hundreds of miles. He saw much land that had never before been seen by white men.

When he was about 200 miles from the mouth of the river, Father Marquette learned that the river did not flow into the Pacific Ocean. He learned that it flowed into the Gulf of Mexico. This was not a route to the Far East after all. Father Marquette and his companions paddled back up the river. This was hard work because they were going against the current.

There were two reasons why Father Marquette and Louis Joliet decided against continuing down the Mississippi River. Some friendly Indians had warned them that warlike tribes lived farther south. Anyway by then they could see that this river was not leading them across the continent as they had hoped it would.

Their Indian friends told the explorers about a shorter way back to the Great Lakes. Father and his party tried it. They paddled their canoes into the Illinois River and up the river until it got too shallow. Then they carried their canoes across a strip of land to another river. A place where canoes or goods are carried is called a portage.

This river flowed into Lake Michigan and brought the explorers to the end of their journey. Louis Joliet hurried back to Quebec to report to the Governor of New France.

The news of the explorations of Father Marquette and Joliet was important to the French. These two French men had gone deep into the middle of the North American continent. No white men had ever been there before. This trip gave France the right to claim much of the Mississippi Valley and the chance to profit from the rich fur trade there. Less than a hundred years later France and England fought a war for the eastern part of this territory called the Ohio Valley.

Father Marquette's Death. The trip down the Mississippi and back had been too much for Father Marquette. He was ill and he was still a long way from his mission at Saint Ignace. He did not

10. The French Settle in the North

want to die without seeing all his Indian friends once more. So Father sent word to them to meet him at a big Indian village near by. They had no telephones or telegraph or even mail trucks then, so Indian runners carried the message.

It was Holy Thursday when the big meeting took place. Six hundred camp fires were burning. That shows how many Indians answered the "Black Robe's" invitation. Father used his last strength teaching the Indians to love God and one another and to live in peace. He said Mass for them on Easter Sunday and then sadly said good-bye.

A group of his Indian friends started out with Father for Saint Ignace. They

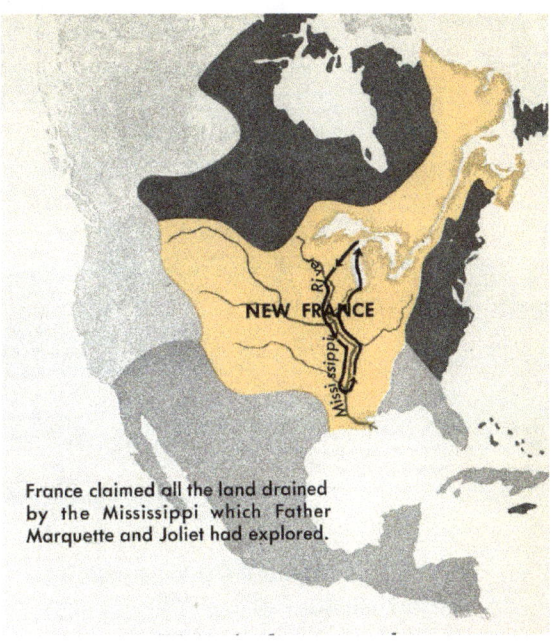

France claimed all the land drained by the Mississippi which Father Marquette and Joliet had explored.

had to travel very slowly because the priest was very weak. Finally Father could go no farther. With his last breath, he praised God and prayed for his Indian friends. The Indians buried him near a river which is now called after him. The next spring the Indians carried the body to the mission at Saint Ignace. There, two Jesuits said the prayers for the dead and buried Father Marquette's body under the little mission chapel.

Father Marquette was one of the many hundreds of priests, Brothers, and Sisters who left their happy homes in Europe and brought Christ and His Blessed Lady to America. Their example has been followed to our day.

La Salle Reaches the Mouth of the Mississippi River. Robert de La Salle was born in France. He came to New France when he was a young man. He loved North America. Father Hennepin, a Franciscan, went with La Salle on some of his trips around the Great Lakes.

"The more I see of this country the more I like it," La Salle wrote to his family in France.

La Salle also loved France, the country where he had been born. He wanted to make France powerful in the New World. La Salle heard that Father Marquette had explored most of the Mississippi River. This gave him an idea.

"I would like to explore the Mississippi River, too," said La Salle. "But I would like to go farther than Father Marquette. I would like to go all the way to the mouth of the river. Then I would claim the whole Mississippi Valley for France. I would also like to build forts along the Mississippi River. The soldiers in these forts would protect the Mississippi Valley and keep it for France."

La Salle went to France. He told the King of France about his plan. The King thought La Salle's plan was a good one. He agreed to help La Salle.

La Salle then went back to New France. It took him many months to get ready for the trip. At last he started down the Illinois River toward the Mississippi. He had 23 Frenchmen and about 30 Indians with him. Their canoes floated hundreds of miles. They marveled as the

10. The French Settle in the North

Mississippi River grew wider and wider. The weather also became warmer. The men saw plants that grow only in the southern part of our country.

One day La Salle noticed that the water was salty. He knew he was near the sea. Then the men saw before them the waters of the Gulf of Mexico. La Salle had traveled all the way from the Great Lakes to the Gulf of Mexico. He was the first man from Europe to do it. This was in the year 1682.

La Salle set up a large wooden cross. He claimed the entire Mississippi Valley for the King of France. He named the land "Louisiana" in honor of King Louis the Fourteenth.

La Salle Tries to Start a Settlement. La Salle returned to France. The French King gave La Salle four ships. He told him to start a settlement at the mouth of the Mississippi River. La Salle's four ships crossed the Atlantic. They sailed into the Gulf of Mexico, but missed the mouth of the Mississippi River. They landed on the coast of Texas.

Here La Salle had many troubles. His men were attacked by the Indians. Some of the men took sick and died. There was not enough food. La Salle decided to go to Quebec for help. With 17 men and five horses, he started on the long, dangerous trip. The men begged La Salle to turn back, but he would not. In March he was killed by one of his own men.

The settlement on the coast of Texas did not last very long. Some of the settlers died. Others were captured by the Indians.

La Salle had carried out part of his plan. He had reached the mouth of the Mississippi River. He had claimed the vast Mississippi Valley for France. But he had not been able to build any forts or start any settlements along the Mississippi River.

Some years after La Salle died, the French did build some forts along the Mississippi River. They also started a small settlement at its mouth. This settlement grew into the city of New Orleans.

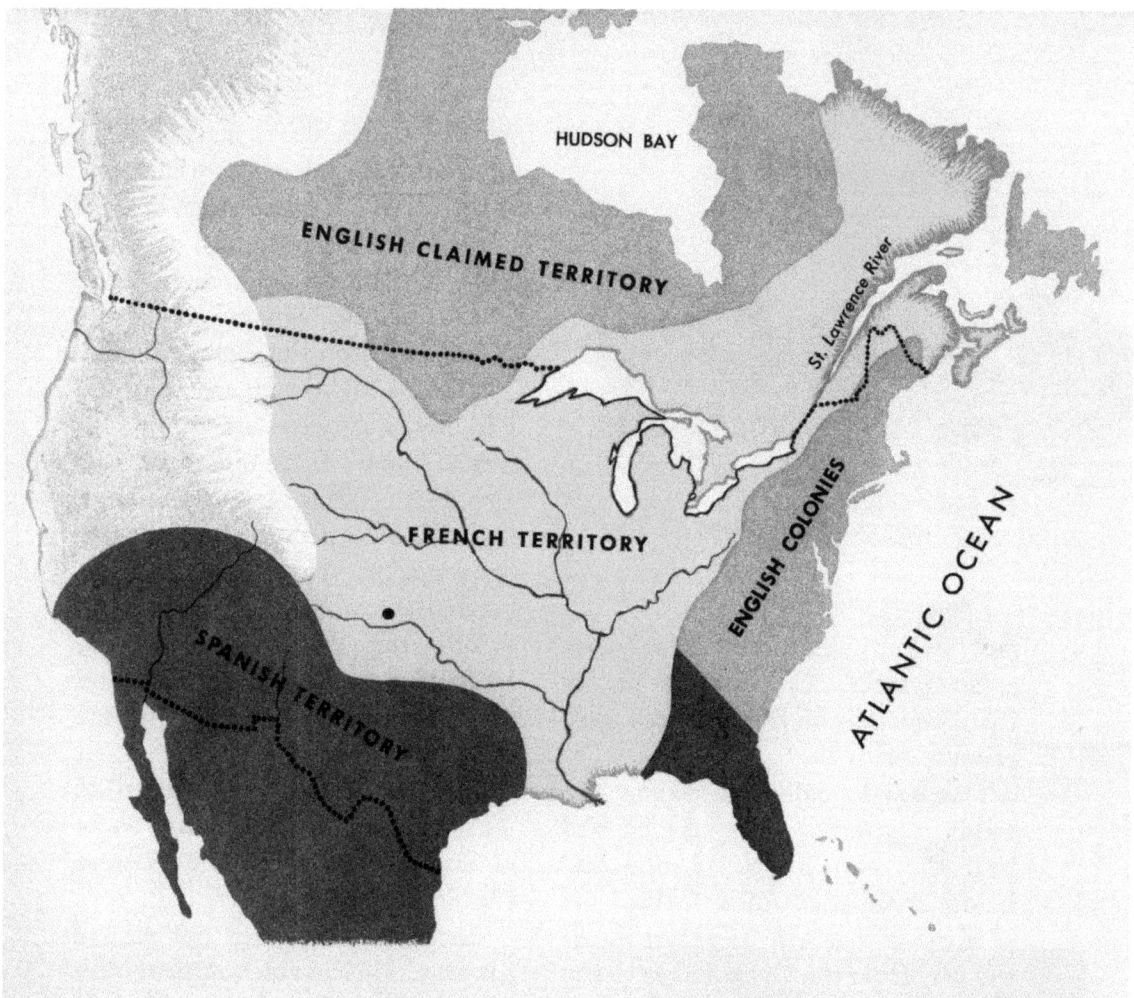

NORTH AMERICA IN 1700

Spain, France, England, Holland, and Sweden once owned parts of the United States. Sweden and Holland lost their shares before 1700.

The map shows the land owned by the French, Spanish, and English in 1700. As you can see, Spain and France owned most of North America. But it was the English colonies which later grew into our country, the United States of America.

10. The French Settle in the North

STUDY LESSON

WHO AM I? Write the name of each person listed. Next to it write the sentence which tells you about the person.

    1. Verrazano 3. Marquette 5. Jogues
    2. Cartier   4. Champlain 6. LaSalle

a. I am called the "Father of New France."
b. I was the first explorer to claim North America for France.
c. I named the Saint Lawrence River.
d. I found that the Mississippi did not run to the Pacific Ocean.
e. I was killed by the Iroquois.
f. I tried to build forts along the Mississippi to keep it for France.

WHAT AM I? Write after each word the phrase that explains it.

    1. Louisiana   3. Iroquois
    2 New Orleans 4. Hurons

a. a tribe of Indians friendly to the French.
b. a part of the United States named after a French king.
c. a city at the mouth of the Mississippi River.
d. a tribe of Indians unfriendly to the French.

WORDS TO KNOW. Use each of the following words in a sentence. Look them up in your dictionary if you are not sure of the meaning.

    armor   current   Jesuit
    trading post mangled canonized

WHERE IS IT? Write each place name and after it the sentence which tells you something about it.

    1. Quebec   3. Lake Champlain
    2. Jamestown 4. Newfoundland

a. Around this coast there was excellent fishing.
b. This town was the first permanent French settlement.
c. This body of water was named after a French explorer.
d. This town was the first permanent English settlement.

DATES TO REMEMBER. Write each date in column A. Next to it write the phrase in column B that matches the date.

A	B
1682	a. the first permanent French settlement.
1608	b. the first journey from the Great Lakes to the Mississippi.

SOMETHING TO THINK ABOUT. Think carefully before you answer these questions.

1. Why do you think Father Isaac Jogues wanted to return to a country where he had suffered so much?
2. Why did French fishermen come to the New World?
3. Why did the French lose their lands in the New World?

11. The Dutch Settle in New York

Henry Hudson Visits New York Harbor. Henry Hudson's ship sailed into New York Harbor in the fall of 1609. The name of his ship was the *Half Moon.*

The Indians on Manhattan Island looked at the ship in surprise. They had never seen anything like this before. Was it a giant bird they wondered. Or perhaps it was a floating house.

Some of the Indians got into their canoes. In the picture above, we see some very curious Indians paddling out to the ship.

Henry Hudson invited the Indians to come aboard his ship. He gave them presents. He showed them about the ship. The Indians were satisfied. They paddled back to shore.

Hudson was sailing for a group of merchants who lived in Holland. The merchants wanted him to find a route to the Far East. It was while he was searching for this route that he sailed into New York Harbor.

Henry Hudson Discovers a River and a Bay. Hudson found a large river flowing into the harbor. We call it the

11. The Dutch Settle in New York

The next year Hudson again sailed to North America. This time he was sailing for an English Company. On this voyage he discovered Hudson Strait and Hudson Bay. For some reason, Hudson's men turned against him. They put him and his son in a small boat. The boat was set adrift on the waters of Hudson Bay. Nothing more was ever heard of Henry Hudson.

Some of the men who did this terrible thing were killed by the Eskimos. The others were arrested when they returned to England.

These two voyages of Henry Hudson were very important. Holland claimed all the land he discovered on his first voyage. England claimed all the land he discovered on his second voyage.

Hudson River today, because it was discovered by Henry Hudson.

Hudson was happy when he found this river. He thought that perhaps there might be a way to sail through North America to the Far East. He sailed up the river. This was the most beautiful country he had ever seen. After he had sailed about 150 miles the water became shallow. He could not sail any farther. So he turned around and went back. He was disappointed because he had not found a route to the Far East.

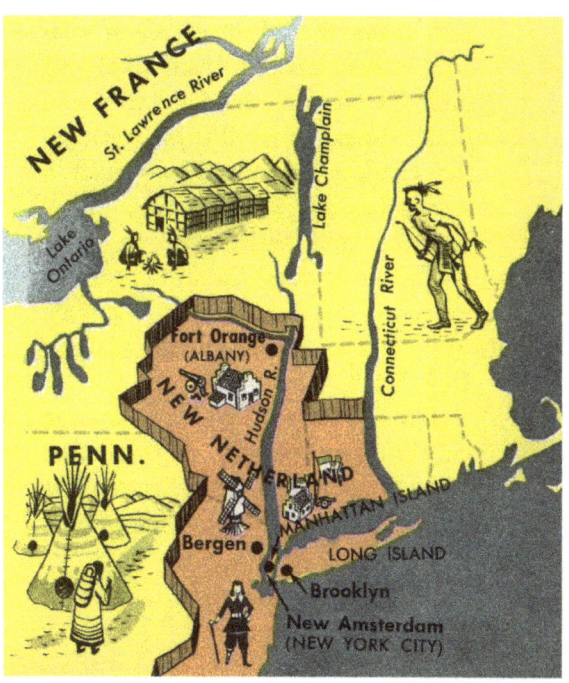

EARLY DUTCH

In 1623 the Dutch started the Colony of New Netherland. A few families settled on Manhattan Island and opened a trading post. In 1626 they paid the Indians $24 for the Island. The Indians thought they were only giving the white men the right to live on and share their land.

The Dutch Settle in New Netherland. The land which the Dutch claimed in North America was called New Netherland. The Dutch West Indies Company sent men to New Netherland to buy furs from the Indians. These men started trading posts on Manhattan Island and along the Hudson River. In 1624 some people from Holland came to New Netherland to make their homes. Most of them went up the Hudson River. They built a fort and called it Fort Orange. This was the first settlement in New Netherland. Fort Orange later became the City of Albany. Today, Albany is the capital of the state of New York.

The second settlement was made on Manhattan Island. It was called New Amsterdam. New Amsterdam was a small town with only a few houses, but it has grown into the great City of New York.

Peter Minuit was the first governor of New Netherland. In 1626 he bought Manhattan Island from the Indians. He gave the Indians about 24 dollars worth of beads, buttons, and ribbons to pay for the island.

Not all the people of New Netherland lived in the settlements. Many of them lived on farms along the Hudson River.

These farms were owned by men called patroons. The patroons were very powerful. They were the rulers and judges of the people who lived on their land. Some patroons were wise and good. Others were very stern and unfair to the farmers.

This was different from the English colonies. In the English colonies each family had its own farm.

SETTLEMENTS

The fur trade made the Dutch colonists rich. New Netherland was in a good place for the fur trade. The Hudson and Mohawk rivers gave the traders a good means of going to and from the inland country where the animals were trapped. Even before the settlers came to Manhattan a few fur traders had built Fort Nassau as an outpost for the fur trade.

Mink, otter, beaver, wild cat, and muskrat were plentiful in this region. Kings, and queens and rich people in Europe were glad to pay high prices for fur cloaks and hats, muffs and capes and carriage blankets. They had bought so many of them that the animals were already becoming hard to find as early as 1800.

The Indians trapped the animals, took off their fur skins, called pelts, and brought them to the trading post. There they traded their costly catch for cloth, liquor (which the Indians called "fire water"), gun powder, and cheap jewelry. This kind of trade in which no money is used is called barter. The white men made too large a profit in the fur trade.

A few years later, in 1664, the English took over the Dutch lands along the Hudson-Mohawk rivers. Then English colonists got rich in the fur trade there. But soon few animals were left in the New York area. The best trapping lands were now farther west around the Great Lakes and Ohio River. This was French territory. The English were jealous. They fought the French and Indian War to get this land.

Swedes Settle at the Mouth of the Delaware. In the same year that Henry Hudson explored New York Harbor he also explored Delaware Bay. He claimed the bay and the land around it for the Dutch.

The Dutch built a settlement on Delaware Bay in 1631. The settlement was destroyed by the Indians.

The next settlers were not from Holland but from Sweden. The Swedish settlers were led by Peter Minuit. This was the same man who had bought Manhattan Island for the Dutch. In 1639, Peter Minuit built a fort and called it Fort Christina. It was named for Queen Christina of Sweden. Fort Christina later grew into the City of Wilmington, Delaware. Philadelphia, Pennsylvania, is also located on land that was once owned by the Swedes. Philadelphia is the third largest city in our country today.

The Swedes also built other settlements near Delaware Bay. They called their colony New Sweden.

The Swedes were the first people in America to build houses out of logs. Later, there were many log cabins in the western part of our country. This style of building is now used for inns and cabins.

There was trouble between the Swedes in New Sweden and the Dutch in New Netherland. Peter Stuyvesant was the governor of New Netherland. We shall read about Peter Stuyvesant again later in

11. The Dutch Settle in New York

this book. In 1655, Peter Stuyvesant sent seven warships to New Sweden. They captured Fort Christina. For the next nine years the Swedish settlements were ruled by the Dutch in New Netherland. Then both New Netherland and New Sweden were captured by the English. All this eastern region fell into the hands of English colonists.

The Dutch and Swedes Owned Valuable Land. The Dutch and the Swedes did not own as much land in North America as the Spanish and French did. But the land they owned was very valuable. The Dutch owned New York Harbor. This is the best harbor along the Atlantic coast. Today, it is the busiest harbor in the world. The Dutch town of New Amsterdam became New York City. This is the largest city in the world. The Hudson River Valley is one of the richest valleys in the world. Fort Orange became Albany. Today, Albany is the capital of the state of New York.

NEW SWEDEN

THE SWEDES SETTLED IN DELAWARE NEAR THE PRESENT CITY OF WILMINGTON. THE DUTCH, ENGLISH, AND QUAKERS IN TURN RULED OVER THIS TERRITORY.

WHERE THE SWEDES LANDED

STUDY LESSON

WHO AM I? Write the name of each person listed. Next to it write the sentence which tells you about the person.

1. Henry Hudson 2. Peter Minuit
3. Peter Stuyvesant

a. I was the first governor of New Netherland.
b. I was the governor of New Netherland who fought the Swedes.
c. I have a river in New York State named after me.

WHAT AM I? Make a list of the following words and write after each of them the phrase that tells you about them.

1. *Half Moon*   2. Fort Orange
3. Fort Christina   4. New Amsterdam

a. the settlement that became Wilmington, Delaware.
b. the settlement that became the largest city in the world.
c. the settlement that became the capital of New York State.
d. the first ship to sail up the Hudson River.

WORDS TO KNOW. Use each of the following words in a sentence. Look them up in your dictionary if you are not sure of the meaning.

harbor   patroon   shallow

WHERE IS IT? Write the name of each place and after it the phrase which tells you something about it.

1. Hudson Bay   2. Hudson River
3. Sweden   4. Delaware

a. a country of Europe.
b. a river in New York State.
c. a body of water named after its discoverer.
d. a settlement made by Swedes.

DATES TO REMEMBER. Write each date in column A. Next write the phrase in column B it matches.

A	B
1. 1609	a. the Swedes settle at Fort Christina.
2. 1626	b. the purchase of Manhattan from the Indians.
3. 1639	c. the arrival of Henry Hudson at New York.

SOMETHING TO THINK ABOUT. Think carefully before you answer these questions.

1. Why were people in the English colonies better treated than those under the Dutch system?
2. What are some things that might have been different about your life if the Dutch had become the rulers of this country?

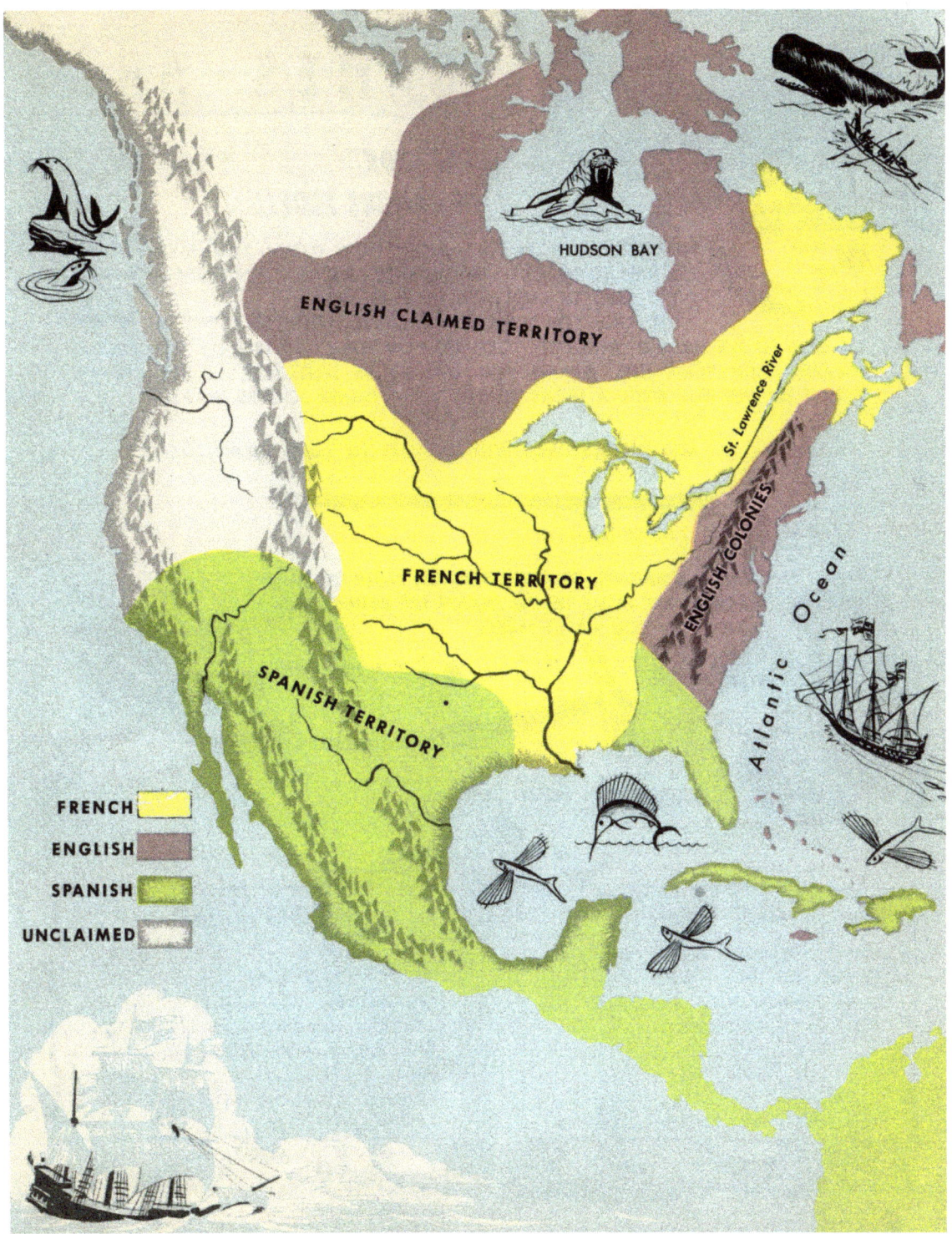

GAMES · ART

SCRAPBOOK OF FAMOUS PEOPLE

SUPPOSE YOU WERE JOHN SMITH. HOW WOULD YOU HAVE GOTTEN THE MEN TO WORK? WRITE A STORY ABOUT JOHN SMITH SHOWING WHAT KIND OF MAN YOU THINK HE WAS.

SUPPOSE YOU WERE A MISSIONARY PRIEST BRINGING THE WORD OF GOD TO THE INDIANS, AND THEY TORTURED YOU FOR YOUR TROUBLE. YOU BARELY ESCAPED WITH YOUR LIFE. WOULD YOU ASK TO BE SENT BACK TO TRY AGAIN? FATHER JOGUES DID. WRITE A STORY TELLING WHAT FATHER JOGUES WAS LIKE.

ADD THESE STORIES WITH PICTURES TO YOUR SCRAPBOOK.

THINGS FROM LONG AGO

USING CARDBOARD OR CONSTRUCTION PAPER OR PAPIER MÂCHÉ, MAKE SOME THINGS WHICH THE INDIANS MIGHT HAVE USED. YOU MIGHT MAKE:

1. A MASK FOR A WAR DANCE
2. A HEADDRESS
3. A HATCHET
4. A VASE WITH INDIAN DESIGNS

NAME GAME

USING PERSONS WHO HAVE APPEARED IN UNIT TWO, PLAY THE GAME WHICH WAS DESCRIBED AT THE END OF UNIT ONE.

FAMOUS PLACES

DRAW OR TRACE A MAP OF NORTH AMERICA AND LABEL MEXICO CITY, GUADALUPE, ST. AUGUSTINE, NEW ORLEANS, JAMESTOWN, NEW YORK CITY, THE HUDSON RIVER, LAKE CHAMPLAIN, THE GREAT LAKES, MONTREAL, QUEBEC, HUDSON BAY, AND THE MISSISSIPPI RIVER.

BOOKS · PLAYS

THIS IS HOW IT HAPPENED

PLAN A PLAY CALLED "BLACK ROBE BRAVERY."

SCENE I: FATHER JOGUES ARRIVES IN AMERICA AND GOES TO LIVE AMONG THE IROQUOIS

SCENE II: THE IROQUOIS FIRST LISTEN BUT LATER BEGIN TO TORTURE FATHER JOGUES

SCENE III: FATHER JOGUES ESCAPES AND RETURNS TO FRANCE

SCENE IV: FATHER JOGUES DESCRIBES AMERICA TO HIS SUPERIORS AND ASKS TO BE SENT BACK TO THE NEW WORLD

SCENE V: FATHER JOGUES IS PUT TO DEATH BY THE IROQUOIS

IT'S FUN TO DRAW

HERE IS A CHANCE TO USE YOUR IMAGINATION.

CAN YOU IMAGINE THE SCENE WHEN JOHN SMITH WAS ABOUT TO BE PUT TO DEATH BY THE INDIANS? DRAW A PICTURE OF HOW YOU THINK THE SCENE MIGHT HAVE LOOKED.

CAN YOU IMAGINE THE FEAR AND SURPRISE OF THE IROQUOIS WHEN THEY HEARD THE NOISE OF CHAMPLAIN'S GUN? DRAW A PICTURE OF THIS LITTLE BATTLE.

EXPLORER'S INFORMATION CENTER

WOULD YOU LIKE TO KNOW MORE ABOUT THE EXPLORERS YOU MET IN THIS UNIT? YOU WILL FIND THESE BOOKS MAKE EXCITING READING.

AULAIRE	POCAHONTAS	DOUBLEDAY
AVERILL	VOYAGES OF JACQUES CARTIER	VIKING
COFFMAN AND GOODMAN	FAMOUS EXPLORERS	DODD
DUVOISIN	FOUR CORNERS OF THE WORLD	KNOPF
STEVENSON	HOLE IN THE DIKE AND OTHER PLAYS ("POCAHONTAS AND CAPTAIN SMITH"; "POCAHONTAS SAVES JAMESTOWN")	HOUGHTON
FOX	THEY SAILED AND SAILED	DUTTON

Unit Three
THIRTEEN GROWING COLONIES

LOOKING INTO THE LONG AGO

Dick was on his way to the big city. He was going to visit his cousin, Mary Jean. His mother and father had just said goodbye to him as he got on the bus. Now he was looking for a seat.

Dick saw a boy about his own age looking out the window. There was an empty seat next to the boy.

"Do you mind if I sit here?" Dick asked.

The boy looked around and smiled. "Oh, no," he said. "Please do."

There was something just a little different about the way the boy talked. He did not sound exactly like the boys Dick knew. But he was very friendly. Dick liked him right away. The boy said his name was Tom.

Dick told Tom about the farm. He told Tom about his school. Then he said, "Now tell me about yourself."

"Well I have lived in Europe up until now."

"Tell me about some of the places you have seen," said Dick.

After they had talked for a while Dick said, "How long have you been in the United States?"

"About six weeks," said Tom.

Dick was puzzled. "You certainly speak our language very well for being here such a short time."

Tom smiled. "I should be able to speak English rather well. You see, I am from England."

Dick was so surprised for a minute that he did not know what to say. Then he began to laugh.

"That is a good joke on me. You said you came from Europe, and I was thinking that everyone in Europe spoke a different language than ours. I forgot all about England."

Mary Jean and her father, Mr. Davis, were waiting for Dick at the bus station. As the three got into Mr. Davis's car, Dick told about the boy he had met on the bus. Then he told what he had said to the boy.

Mr. Davis laughed. "Tom must have been very polite. He could have told you that the English people had the language long before the Americans."

"Dad," said Mary Jean, "why is it that almost all Americans speak English? We learned in history that the Spaniards, French, and Dutch all owned parts of our country at one time. Why don't we speak Spanish, French, or Dutch?"

"Well," said Mr. Davis, "Spanish is spoken by the people of Mexico, Central America, and much of South America."

"In one part of Canada," said Mr. Davis, "most of the people speak French. That is because so many French people settled there. But not so many French settled in our country."

"Most of the first settlers in our part of North America must have been English," Mary Jean said.

"Yes," her father answered. "It was the thirteen English colonies that became the United States of America."

"In that history show, I was one of the Jamestown settlers," Dick said. "I guess I was one of those who brought the English language to America."

"It's true that we owe our language to the first English settlers," said Mr. Davis. "But we also owe them much more than that."

"If we owe so much to the English settlers," said Dick, "I suppose we will spend some time this year learning about them."

"I think you will," said Mr. Davis. "Well we are almost home."

"And I see Aunt Nell standing in the doorway," said Dick.

"We will be just in time for lunch," Mary Jean said, "and Mother has your favorite dessert."

"I have so many favorite desserts, I cannot imagine what it is," said Dick. "But don't tell me. I want to be surprised."

12. Pilgrims and Puritans Come to New England

Many English People Suffered for Their Religion. The soldiers are taking these people to prison.

Why do these people have to go to prison? Because the soldiers caught them going to their own church instead of going to the Church of England.

At one time almost everybody in England was a Catholic. Then a King of England left the Catholic Church. A new church was started— the Church of England. The King of England was the head of this church. Other new churches were also started. The people who belonged to all these new churches were called Protestants because they protested against the Catholic Church.

A law was passed in England that everyone must belong to the Church of England. People who tried to go to any other church were arrested. Sometimes they had to pay a fine. Sometimes they had to go to prison.

Who are the people in the picture? Perhaps they are Catholics. The Catholics knew that their Church was the One True

12. Pilgrims and Puritans Come to New England

Church. They would not join the Church of England. The Catholics in England had to suffer much for their Faith.

Or perhaps the people in the picture are Protestants who do not belong to the Church of England. There were many different kinds of Protestants in England. The Protestants who did not belong to the Church of England also had to suffer for their religion.

Today, in our country we have freedom of religion. This means that there is no law telling us what church we must attend. No soldiers will take us to jail for going to our own church. There was no such freedom of religion in England in the 1600's and 1700's.

Many people left England and came to America. They hoped that in America they would be able to go to their own churches without being arrested.

In this chapter we shall read about the Pilgrims and the Puritans. Both the Pilgrims and the Puritans were Protestants who suffered for their religion. They left England and came to America so they could worship God in the way they thought was right.

The Pilgrims Come to America. William Bradford was one of the Protestants who did not belong to the Church of England. He lived in the village of Scrooby, in England. When William was seventeen years old, the minister of his church was arrested.

William heard some of the men talking.

"If we stay here, we shall be arrested over and over again," the men said. "We must leave England. Let's go to Holland."

William went to Holland with the others. He was about 18 years old. In Holland, he learned to be a silk weaver.

But the English people were not happy in Holland. In England they had been farmers. They could not buy farms in Holland, so they had to live in the big cities. They found that it was hard for them to make a living in Holland.

They also found that their children were speaking Dutch instead of English. They were afraid their children would forget their English ways.

"Let's go to America," some of the people said. "There is plenty of land in America. We can start farms there. Also, we shall be able to keep our English language and our English ways."

These people were poor. They could not buy a ship or the things they needed to start a settlement. They borrowed the money from some merchants. They agreed to pay back the money after they started their farms in America.

When it was time to sail, only 35 of the people left Holland. William Bradford was one of them. It was about this time that the people were first called Pilgrims.

When the Pilgrims got to England they were joined by 67 others. These 102 people sailed from England in September, 1620. They sailed on a ship called the *Mayflower*.

The *Mayflower* sailed through many storms. At times it seemed the waves would batter the little ship to pieces. The Pilgrims were often sea-sick and cold. It took the ship 63 days to cross the Atlantic. Today, fast steamers make the same trip in four or five days.

The Pilgrims were supposed to go to Virginia. They missed Virginia and came to land farther north. This is the land that we today call Massachusetts.

A Hard Winter at Plymouth. Before they landed the Pilgrims had a meeting. The men in the party signed an agreement. This agreement is called the Mayflower Compact. The men said they would obey all the laws made for the colony. They elected John Carver to be their governor.

The Pilgrims explored the coast. They were looking for a place to build a settlement. They came to a fine harbor. Captain John Smith had discovered this harbor a few years earlier. He had named it Plymouth, after the city of Plymouth in England. The Pilgrims decided to build their settlement at Plymouth. The Pilgrims finally landed on December 10, 1620. They knelt and thanked God for a safe landing.

It was very, very cold when the Pilgrims landed. They were not used to such cold winters. Many of them were still tired and sick from the long ocean voyage. It was too late in the year to plant crops, so they had little food. More than half the Pilgrims died that first winter. At one time there were only six or seven persons who were well. These six or seven people had to take care of the sick, and they had to bury the dead. John Carver, the governor, died during that first winter. William Bradford was elected to take his place. Bradford was governor of the colony for 31 years.

The First Thanksgiving. In the spring an Indian came walking into the settlement. The Pilgrims were amazed when he said, "Welcome!" He had learned a little English from fishermen who had visited Maine. His name was Samoset.

Later, Samoset brought another Indian named Squanto. Squanto could speak more English than Samoset could. Squanto taught the Pilgrims how to plant corn. He told them the best places to go fishing and hunting.

One day Squanto came to Plymouth with a great chief named Mas- sasoit. Massasoit made a treaty with the Pilgrims. In this treaty the Pilgrims and Indians said they would be friends. The Indians and the Pilgrims lived in peace for many years after that.

At the end of the first summer the Pilgrims had many things to be thankful for. They now had houses to protect them from the weather. They had raised enough corn to last them through the winter. They were at peace with the Indians. The Pilgrims knew that everything they had they owed to God. They decided to have a thanksgiving celebration.

Massasoit came with ninety Indians. They brought seven deer which they had shot in the forest. The Pilgrims supplied wild turkeys, corn, and pumpkins. The Pilgrims prayed and thanked God for helping them. Then they sat down with the Indians to a great feast. This was the first Thanksgiving. Today we celebrate Thanksgiving on the fourth Thursday of every November.

12. Pilgrims and Puritans Come to New England

The Pilgrims got along well. They sent fish, furs, and lumber to England. In a few years they had paid back the money which they had borrowed from the merchants.

More people came to the colony. By 1643 there were 3,000 settlers in Plymouth.

The Puritans Come to America. Another group of English Protestants were called Puritans. Like the Pilgrims, they wished to come to America to worship God in their own way. The Puritans formed the Massachusetts Bay Company.

In 1628 the Massachusetts Bay Company sent a small group of settlers to North America. They started the village of Salem.

In 1630 about 1000 people from England came to the Massachusetts Bay Colony. They brought cattle, horses, seed, and tools. These people built their settlement at the mouth of the Charles River. The settlement later became known as Boston. John Winthrop was the leader of the Puritans who founded Boston. He became the first governor of the Colony.

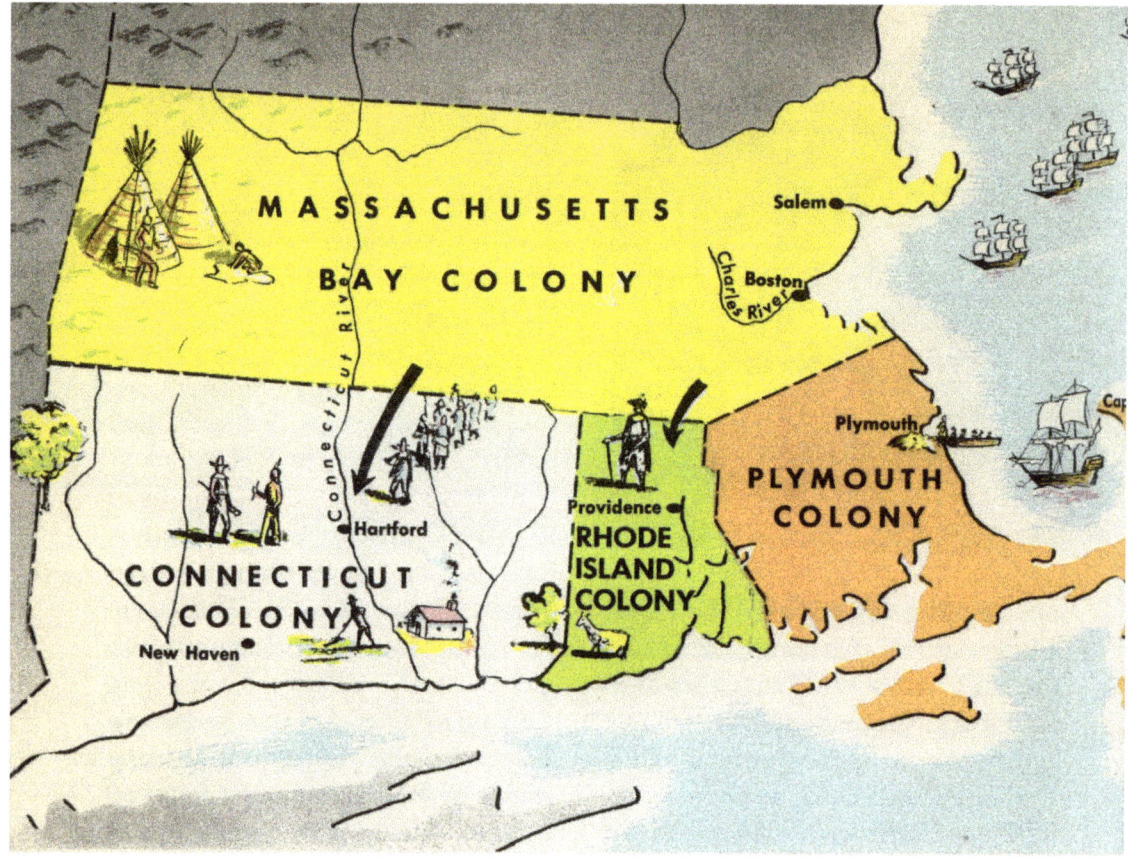

Between 1630 and 1640 many ships came to the Massachusetts Bay Colony. It grew faster than the near-by Plymouth Colony. By 1640 there were about 26,000 people in the colony. They had built many villages along the coast.

The Puritans left England because they did not want to be forced to belong to the Church of England. But in Massachusetts, they forced other people to accept their religion. Everyone was supposed to go to the Puritan Church whether he was a Puritan or not. Everyone was forced to give money to the Puritan Church.

Only Puritans were allowed to vote or to hold office. People who were not Puritans found that life was not very pleasant in the Massachusetts Bay Colony.

In 1690 the King of England ordered that Plymouth Colony and the Massachusetts Bay Colony should be combined into one colony. The new larger colony was called Massachusetts.

Roger Williams Founds Rhode Island. Roger Williams was a minister in Salem. He said some things that the Puritan leaders did not like.

He said that the Puritans had no right to force everyone to go to their church.

Roger Williams also said the land in North America belonged to the Indians. He said that the Puritans had no right to live in Massachusetts Bay Colony, unless the Indians gave them permission.

The Puritan leaders said that nobody would be allowed to say such things in their colony. They said that Roger Williams must go back to England. They sent soldiers to arrest him.

Roger Williams escaped into the forest before the soldiers could catch him. It was the middle of winter.

The snow was deep and the weather was bitterly cold. Roger Williams pushed on. He reached the camp of his Indian friend, Chief Massasoit. By this time Williams was very sick. The Indians took care of him until he got better.

In the spring, Roger Williams started out on his travels once more. He found a place he thought would be good for a settlement. He bought the land from the Indians.

Roger Williams started a settlement which he called Providence. He said that in his settlement people would be allowed to go to whatever church they believed in. Many people from the other colonies moved to Providence.

In time, the settlement of Providence grew into the colony of Rhode Island.

Hooker Settles Connecticut. Thomas Hooker was an important minister in Massachusetts. Like Roger Williams, he did not agree with some of the ideas of the Puritan leaders. He thought everybody should have a voice in the government. The Puritan leaders wanted to control the government of Massachusetts. Thomas Hooker and most of the members of his parish decided to leave Massachusetts.

About a hundred people started out for the Connecticut River. They took their cattle with them. They traveled about seven or eight miles each day. Then they camped for the night.

On the banks of the Connecticut River, Hooker and his followers decided to settle. They bought land from the Indians and cleared it. They built homes, laid out farms and started a village which they called Hartford. Soon, several other villages grew up close by. These became the colony of Connecticut.

The people of Connecticut wanted a good government. They drew up a set of rules for their colony in 1639. These rules were called the Fundamental Orders of Connecticut. The rules gave the people a voice in their government. This was the first written constitution in our history.

What We Mean by New England. People who came to the New World from Europe did not want to forget the countries in which they had been born.

12. Pilgrims and Puritans Come to New England

The Spaniards gave the name New Spain to their land in the New World. The French gave the name New France to the land along the St. Lawrence River. We know that there was also a New Netherland and a New Sweden. In the same way, the English who settled in the northern part of our country called their land New England.

By the year 1700 there were four New England colonies. We have read that the colony of Massachusetts was formed by combining Plymouth Colony and the Massachusetts Bay Colony. We know that Rhode Island and Connecticut were started by settlers from Massachusetts.

The fourth New England colony was New Hampshire. It was also started by people from Massachusetts. New Hampshire was part of Massachusetts for many years. It became a separate colony in 1679.

Today there are six New England states. Why are there six states where there were only four colonies?

PAUL, AN ENGLISH COLONIST

Paul lives in Massachusetts. His parents came from England. Paul belongs to the Puritan Church. There are many Puritans in Massachusetts. In other colonies there are many people belonging to other Protestant churches. There are very few Catholics in the English colonies. The few who are here live mostly in Maryland and Pennsylvania.

Paul owns his house and farm. He can do whatever he wishes with his farm. He votes for members of the assembly. The assembly decides important questions for the colony, for example, what taxes Paul must pay.

It would be wrong, however, to think that the English colonists were completely free. It was dangerous for a man to criticize the king or his officers. Negro slaves and certain kinds of servants had no freedom at all.

We see, then, that the English colonists had more freedom than the other colonists. They also had more freedom than most of the people of Europe. But they did not have as much freedom as we Americans have today.

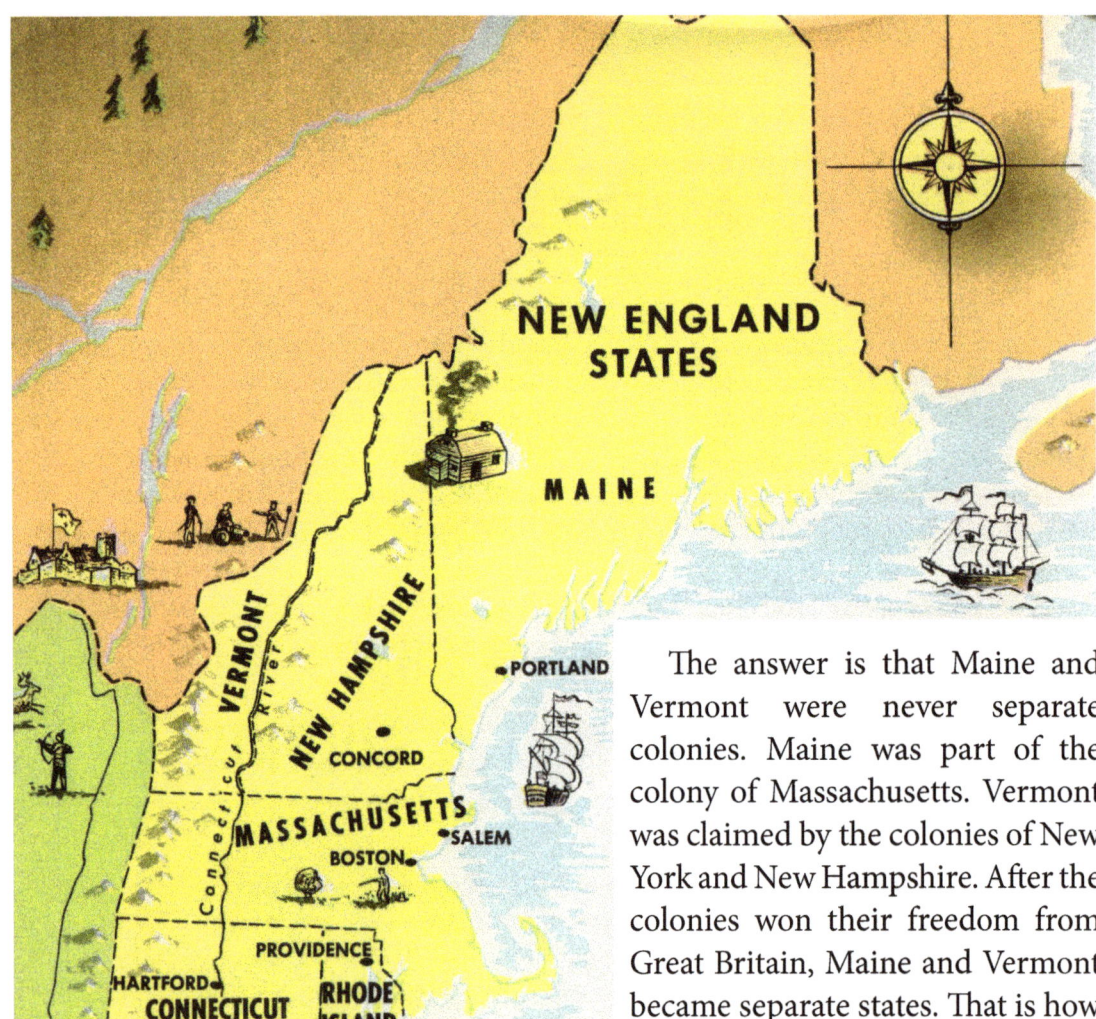

The answer is that Maine and Vermont were never separate colonies. Maine was part of the colony of Massachusetts. Vermont was claimed by the colonies of New York and New Hampshire. After the colonies won their freedom from Great Britain, Maine and Vermont became separate states. That is how four colonies became six states.

STUDY LESSON

WHERE AM I? Answer each question in a complete sentence.

1. Which ocean did the Pilgrims cross to reach America?
2. Name the four New England colonies. Now name six states which came from those four New England colonies.
3. Which New England colonies became states after they won their freedom from Great Britain?
4. What large New England city was founded by the Puritans?

12. Pilgrims and Puritans Come to New England

WHAT AM I? Write each word or name and after it the phrase that explains it.

1. Mayflower
2. settlement
3. Church of England
4. Mayflower Compact
5. The One True Church
6. Puritans

a. an agreement signed by the Pilgrims.
b. the Catholic Church.
c. people had to belong to it by law.
d. the ship that carried the Pilgrims to America.
e. a group of Protestants who did not belong to the Church of England.
f. a place where colonists made their new homes.

WHO AM I? Write each name and after it the phrase that tells about him.

1. Massasoit
2. Roger Williams
3. Thomas Hooker
4. William Bradford
5. Squanto
6. John Winthrop

a. founded the colony of Connecticut.
b. governor of Plymouth Colony.
c. first governor of the Massachusetts Bay Colony.
d. taught the Pilgrims how to plant corn.
e. Indian chief who made a treaty with the Pilgrims.
f. started Providence settlement.

WORDS TO KNOW. Use each of these words in a sentence. Look them up in your dictionary, if you are not sure of their meaning.

harbor	governor	agreement
colony	treaty	merchants

SOMETHING TO THINK ABOUT. Think carefully before you answer these questions.

1. Why do you think the founders of the United States made it a law that the government could not force us to go to church?
2. Do you think it would be a good thing if we had a law that all Americans must go to the Catholic Church?
3. Did the Puritans want to allow everyone to go to whatever church he pleased?

WHAT IS THE REASON? Think carefully before you answer each question.

1. Why did the Pilgrims and the Puritans leave England?
2. Why were the Pilgrims unhappy in Holland?
3. Why did the Pilgrims hold the first Thanksgiving?
4. Why did Roger Williams leave the Massachusetts Bay Colony?
5. Why did Plymouth Colony almost fail?

13. People From Many Countries Come to the Middle Colonies

New Netherland Becomes New York. The man who is tearing up the note in the picture above is Peter Stuyvesant. He is the governor of New Netherland. It is the year 1664.

We read about New Netherland and Peter Stuyvesant in Chapter 11. You remember that New Netherland was the Dutch colony in North America. Peter Stuyvesant was the fourth governor of this colony.

The English had colonies both north and south of New Netherland. The English did not like to have a Dutch colony separating their colonies. The Dutch also had the best harbor along the coast, and the English did not like this.

The English leaders said, "The Dutch have no right to have a colony there. John Cabot claimed all of North America for England."

In the year 1664, three English warships sailed into the harbor of New Amsterdam. The English sent Peter Stuyvesant a note. They asked him to surrender.

In the picture we see Peter Stuyvesant tearing up the note. "I shall never surrender," he said.

The other picture shows what happened next.

When Peter Stuyvesant left, some of the Dutch settlers picked up the pieces of the note. They put the pieces together. They read the note.

13. People From Many Countries Come to the Middle Colonies

"The English say that if we surrender without fighting we shall be allowed to keep our land," said one of these Dutch settlers.

"Peter Stuyvesant is a very stern governor," said another settler.

"The people in the English colonies have more freedom than we do," said a third settler.

The news spread through New Amsterdam. Very few of the people liked the rule of Peter Stuyvesant. They would not fight for him.

So Peter Stuyvesant was forced to surrender without firing a shot. New Netherland became an English colony.

The King of England gave the colony to his brother, the Duke of York. The name New Netherland was changed to New York. The town of New Amsterdam became the town of New York.

Life in New Netherland. At first there were no women in the Dutch colony. Only men came over to trade with the Indians for furs. In 1624 two families came to live in the colony. They decided to settle on Manhattan Island near Fort Amsterdam. Soon there were 270 men, women, and children in the village called New Amsterdam.

The settlers started to build homes and lay out gardens. Dutch people love flowers. No Dutch family could live very long without a pretty garden of waving tulips and other bright flowers. They also planted vegetables to eat.

At first the settlers may have been a little homesick. When they started to build homes they wanted them to look like the houses they had left back home in Holland. They built them close together with long, sloping red roofs. Outside the front door each house had a little platform with steps going up to it. This was called a stoop. These stoops were the very first front porches in America. In summer the Dutch-American families used to sit on their stoops and chat with their neighbors next door.

The front door of a Dutch house was divided in two parts, upper and lower. They opened the top part to let in fresh air. The bottom part was left shut to keep out stray animals.

Unlike early New England houses the Dutch houses had two or three stories. They were made of colored brick. The bricks were yellow and blue and red and brown. They were laid in fancy patterns. Pots of gay flowers sat on the windowsills. The Dutch people were not Puritans. They liked their homes to look pretty.

Inside and out, the Dutch homes were brushed and scrubbed till they shone. The Dutch housewives were famous for cleanliness. The center of family life was the fireplace. The Dutch fireplaces were not plain and simple like the ones in New England. They were made pretty with blue and white tiles with pictures on them. These pictures often told stories from the Bible.

A child could sit by the fire and learn his Bible history by studying the pictures and asking Mother questions about what he saw. Shining pots and pans and kettles were hung around the fireplace.

The Dutch homes had carved chairs and big beds and cupboards with open shelves. Here the housewife showed off her treasures of fine china and glowing pewter and shining silver. Some beds were closed out of sight in the daytime—very modern. Big, colored chests held fluffy piles of fresh towels, linens, blankets, and quilts.

A FAMOUS GOVERNOR OF NEW YORK

In 1682 the Duke of York made Thomas Dongan the governor of New York. Thomas Dongan was a Catholic. In those days it was very unusual for a Catholic to hold office either in England or in the English colonies.

Governor Dongan called together the first assembly in New York. The members of this assembly were elected by the people. They made laws for New York. This was the first time that the people of New York were given a voice in their government.

The first assembly passed a bill called "A Charter of Liberties." The charter said people could go to any church they wished. People could not be punished because of their religion. The charter said that people should always be allowed to elect their own lawmakers. It said that taxes could be made only by lawmakers who were elected by the people.

Governor Dongan was happy with the charter. He signed it and sent it to the Duke of York, in England. The Duke of York signed it, but he did not return it to New York. Therefore, the charter never became law.

The charter was very important even though it did not become law. Later, England used many parts of the charter in ruling her other colonies. Many parts of the charter were used later in the Constitution of New York State and in the Constitution of the United States.

Governor Dongan started the first post office in New York. He built important roads and signed treaties of peace with the Indians.

Thomas Dongan was governor of New York for only five years, but he was one of the greatest governors of colonial days.

New Jersey Becomes a Colony. The Duke of York did not keep all the land tha thad been taken from the Dutch. He gave the land between the Hudson and Delaware rivers to two of his friends. One of these friends was Lord John Berkeley. The other was Sir George Carteret. Sir George had once been the governor of the Island of Jersey. Therefore, he named the colony New Jersey. Neither Berkeley nor Carteret themselves ever came to this country, but Carteret sent his nephew, Philip Carteret, as the first governor of the colony.

In 1664 thirty English settlers came to New Jersey. They laid out a town and called it Elizabethtown. Later it became the city of Elizabeth. Then a band of Puritans who were unahppy in Connecticut came to New Jersey and started a town on the Passaic River. This was to become the city of Newark.

For a number of years the colony was governed by William Penn and a few other Quakers who bought it. While under the Quakers New Jersey kept good faith with the Indians. The people had a voice in the government through their assemblies, and freedom of religion was given to everyone. However in 1702 the colony was taken over by the King of England.

Then Catholics could no longer practice their religion, according to the law. In spite of the law, Father Farmer, New Jersey's first missionary, and

13. People From Many Countries Come to the Middle Colonies

Father Schneider, who was also a doctor, traveled about bringing the Mass and the sacraments to Catholics in the colony.

William Penn and Pennsylvania. An Englishman named George Fox started a new religion in 1647. He called this new religion the Society of Friends. The Friends were usually called Quakers.

The Quakers had a hard time in England. They would not belong to the Church of England. They believed it was wrong to take off their hats even to kings or noblemen. They believed that all war was wrong, and they taught that it was wrong even to join the army. The men who ruled England did not like these ideas. George Fox and his followers were put in prison many times.

The English people were amazed when William Penn became a Quaker. William Penn's father was Admiral Penn, a famous naval officer. The Penn family was very wealthy. Even though he came from a wealthy and well-known family, William Penn was put into prison for his beliefs.

William Penn wished to start a colony where there would be freedom of religion. There the Quakers could live in peace. People who belonged to other religions would also be allowed to live there and worship God in their own ways.

The King owed Admiral Penn a large sum of money. After Admiral Penn died, the king owed this money to William. William Penn asked the king if he would give him some land in America instead of the money. The king was glad to do this. Penn suggested that this land be called Sylvania. This means "woodland." The king put the name Penn in front of this, in honor of his old friend, Admiral

Penn. That is how the colony came to be called Pennsylvania.

Three thousand people came to Penn's colony in 1681. Penn himself came the next year. He laid out a city which he called Philadelphia. This means "City of Brotherly Love."

Penn made friends with the Indians. He and the Indians signed a treaty of peace. As long as Penn lived his settlers had no trouble with the Indians.

These were years of great trouble in Europe. There were many wars. In some countries people were suffering for their religion. Some people did not have work and did not have enough to eat. Many of these people were glad to get away from Europe. Many came to Pennsylvania. They were welcomed by William Penn.

Some people came to Pennsylvania from Germany. In their own country the Germans are called *Deutsch*. The English-speaking people did not pronounce this word correctly. They said "Dutch" instead of "Deutsch." That is why the Germans in Pennsylvania were called the "Pennsylvania Dutch," although they were not Dutch at all.

People also came to Pennsylvania from Scotland, Ireland, and many other places.

Many Catholics came to Pennsylvania. In most of the English colonies Catholics were not allowed to practice their religion, but in Pennsylvania they were. Penn tried to form a true Christian community. He wanted justice, freedom, and kindness to be the rule.

Large groups of German and Dutch settlers came to Pennsylvania in 1685. They settled at a place which they called Germantown which is now part of

13. People From Many Countries Come to the Middle Colonies

Delaware. We have already read that the Swedes settled at the mouth of the Delaware River. They called their colony New Sweden. Later, the Dutch captured New Sweden. Then the English took over all the land ruled by the Dutch. The land that had been New Sweden was then called Delaware.

The Swedes kept on living in Delaware although it was captured first by the Dutch and then by the English. Many other settlers later joined the Swedes.

William Penn was given Delaware because it was across the river from his colony. Delaware was given its own government in 1703.

Philadelphia. These people were skilled weavers, silversmiths, lacemakers, and printers. Before 1690 they built the first paper mill in America.

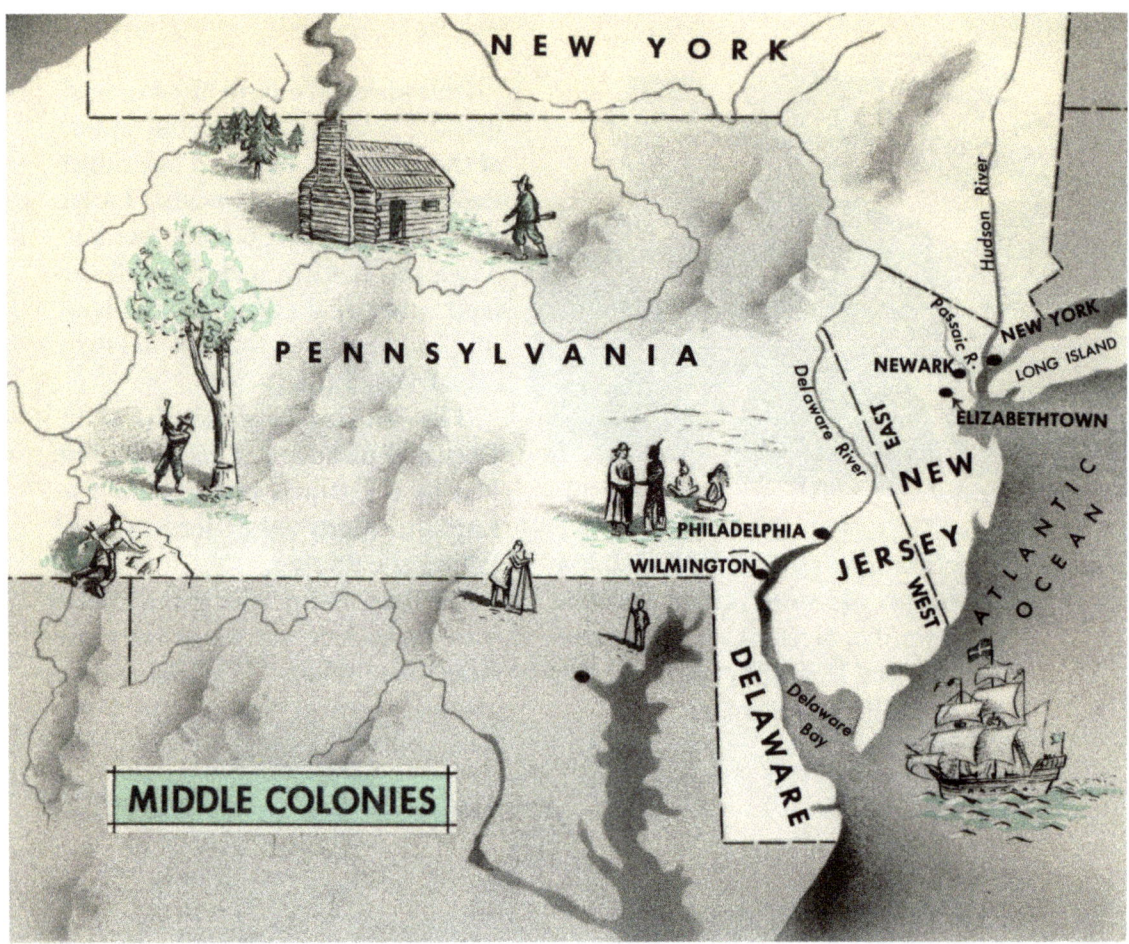

What We Mean by the Middle Colonies. This map shows the four colonies that we read about in this chapter. They are called the Middle Colonies. Do you know why? The reason is that the four New England colonies were to the north of them and the five Southern Colonies were to the south of them. So the Middle Colonies were right in the middle between New England and the South.

In New England almost all the settlers were English. In the Middle Colonies most of the settlers were English, but there were also many settlers from other countries. There were Swedes in Delaware. There were Dutch in New York. There were Germans, Scotch, Irish, and people from many other countries in Pennsylvania. All these people were ruled by English laws. In time, everyone learned to speak English.

13. People From Many Countries Come to the Middle Colonies

STUDY LESSON

WHERE IS IT? Answer each question in a complete sentence.

1. Which state did the Dutch colony of New Netherland become?
2. Which waterway did the Dutch use when they traveled north in their New Netherland colony?
3. What two rivers formed the boundaries of the New Jersey colony?
4. Which city was founded by William Penn?
5. Can you name the Middle Colonies?

WHAT AM I? Write each name and after it the phrase that explains it.

1. New Amsterdam
2. New Sweden
3. Pennsylvania Dutch
4. Quakers
5. Pennsylvania

a. named in honor of Admiral Penn.
b. taught that it was wrong to go to war.
c. later became New York City.
d. came from Germany.
e. later became Delaware.

SOMETHING TO THINK ABOUT. Think carefully before you answer these questions.

1. Do you think Peter Stuyvesant was a good governor?
2. What reasons did the Dutch have for surrendering New Netherland without firing a shot?

WHO AM I? Write each name and after it the phrase that tells about him.

1. Peter Stuyvesant   2. John Cabot
3. Duke of York   4. George Fox
5. Admiral Penn

a. claimed all of North America for England.
b. started the Quaker religion.
c. brother of the King of England.
d. Governor of New Netherland.
e. was given land in America for money owed to him.

WHAT IS THE REASON? Think carefully before you answer each question.

1. Why did the English want the Dutch colony of New Amsterdam?
2. Why did the Quakers leave England to come to Pennsylvania?
3. Why did many Catholics come to Pennsylvania rather than to some of the other English colonies?
4. Why were New York, New Jersey, Pennsylvania, and Delaware called the Middle Colonies?

WORDS TO KNOW. Use each of these words in a sentence. Look them up in your dictionary if you are not sure of their meaning.

surrender   **noblemen**   **freedom**
coast   **laws**   **society**

14. The Southern Colonies

Virginia, First Southern Colony. We have learned how the New England Colonies were founded. Then we found out how the Middle Colonies were started. In this chapter we will read about the Southern Colonies. We have already read about Virginia, the first Southern colony.

We know that the first English settlement in North America was at Jamestown. The colony of Virginia grew from this settlement. For a time, Virginia was the only English colony in North America. Even after the Pilgrims and Puritans settled in New England, there were no colonies close to Virginia.

Then some neighbors moved in near Virginia. The first neighbor was Maryland. This is north of Virginia, as you can see on the map on the next page.

Catholics Come to Maryland. Many of the settlers in this picture are Catholics. They have just arrived on the coast of North America. They have brought two priests with them. One of the priests is saying Mass. He is Father Andrew White. It is March 25, 1634.

Behind the settlers you can see two ships. They are the *Ark* and the *Dove*. These two ships have brought the settlers from England to North America.

The Catholic settlers are happy to be in a place where they can attend Mass. Back in England, people who attended Mass were fined or put into prison. Priests who were caught saying Mass could be put to death.

How did these settlers happen to come to America? This is the way it happened:

14. The Southern Colonies

The first Lord Baltimore was an important man in England. He became a Catholic. He felt sorry for his fellow Catholics. He asked the king if he could start a colony where Catholics would be allowed to practice their religion. The king gave Lord Baltimore a large piece of land north of Virginia. The king said the colony should be called Maryland.

The first Lord Baltimore died before he could start the colony of Maryland. His son, the second Lord Baltimore, decided to carry out his father's plans. He could not come to America, so he sent his brother, Leonard Calvert, to be the governor. Leonard Calvert crossed the ocean with the first settlers. We can see him in the picture above. He and the second priest are kneeling in front of the other settlers.

Religious Freedom in Maryland. Not all settlers who came to live in Maryland were Catholics. Many of them were Protestants. Leonard Calvert said that the Protestants would be allowed to practice their religion. He said there would be freedom of religion in Maryland. Maryland was the first of the English colonies to grant freedom of religion.

You probably remember that Roger Williams said there would be freedom of religion in Rhode Island. Maryland was founded two years before Rhode Island.

At first, everything went well for the settlers. The Indians were friendly. Governor Calvert paid the Indians for the land the settlers were using. An Indian chief gave Father White his own hut to use as a chapel. The Indian braves helped the white men clear the land and

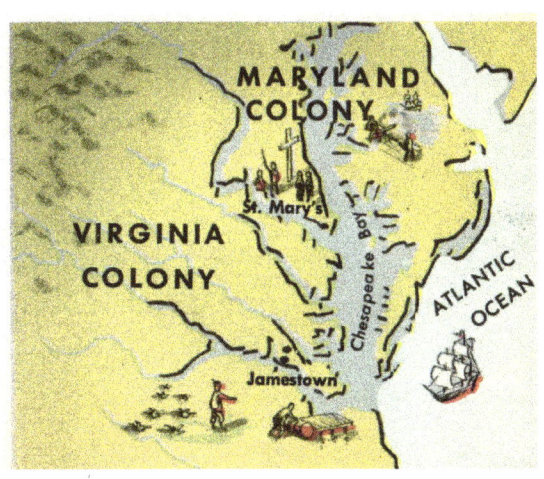

build houses. The squaws taught the women how to make bread out of Indian corn. Like their neighbors in Virginia, the settlers raised tobacco and sent it to England.

In 1649 the people of Maryland passed a new law. This law was called the Toleration Act. It said that every Christian would have freedom of religion. This was a good law, but there was freedom of religion in Maryland even before the law was passed.

Some years later the king said that Maryland would no longer belong to Lord Baltimore. The king said that now Maryland would have to be ruled by the same laws as England. This meant that the Toleration Act would no longer be in effect. After that, the Catholics had much to suffer in the colony that had been started for them.

The Carolinas. South of Virginia the land was very fertile. It was well suited for growing tobacco and rice. Planters from Virginia started to move to this area.

In 1587 Sir Walter Raleigh had sent a party which settled in what later became North Carolina. The settlement did not last, but here the first English child was born in America in 1587. Her name was Virginia Dare.

In 1663 the king gave the land south of Virginia to eight of his friends. This new colony was called Carolina. Later, it was divided into two parts: North Carolina and South Carolina. Settlers built towns at Albemarle and Charles Town.

The first settlement that lasted in South Carolina was made in 1670 and called Charles Town in honor of the king. Trade with the Indians and shipping furs to England made the colony prosper.

Georgia Is Founded in 1733. There were some very strict laws in England. A man who could not pay the money he owed was sent to prison. Sometimes, his whole family were sent to prison with him. The prisons were horrible places. They were cold in the winter and hot in the summer. They were dirty. They had little fresh air. Many of the prisoners took sick and died.

A man named James Oglethorpe visited some of the prisons. He was shocked by what he saw.

"Why punish these people?" he asked. "They have done nothing wrong. It is not their fault if they have no money. This way they will never be able to pay what they owe. They cannot earn money while they are in prison."

James Oglethorpe asked King George for some land in America. He wanted to start a colony for the people who owed debts. There, the people would be able to lead useful lives. This would be much better than keeping them in prison.

King George did not have much land left. But there was a little between South Carolina and Florida. This land was claimed by both England and Spain. King George was afraid some Spaniards from Florida might move into this land. He was glad to give it to James Oglethorpe. In this way, there would be Englishmen instead of Spaniards living on the land.

Oglethorpe started his new colony in 1733. He named it Georgia, in honor of King George II, who was the King of England.

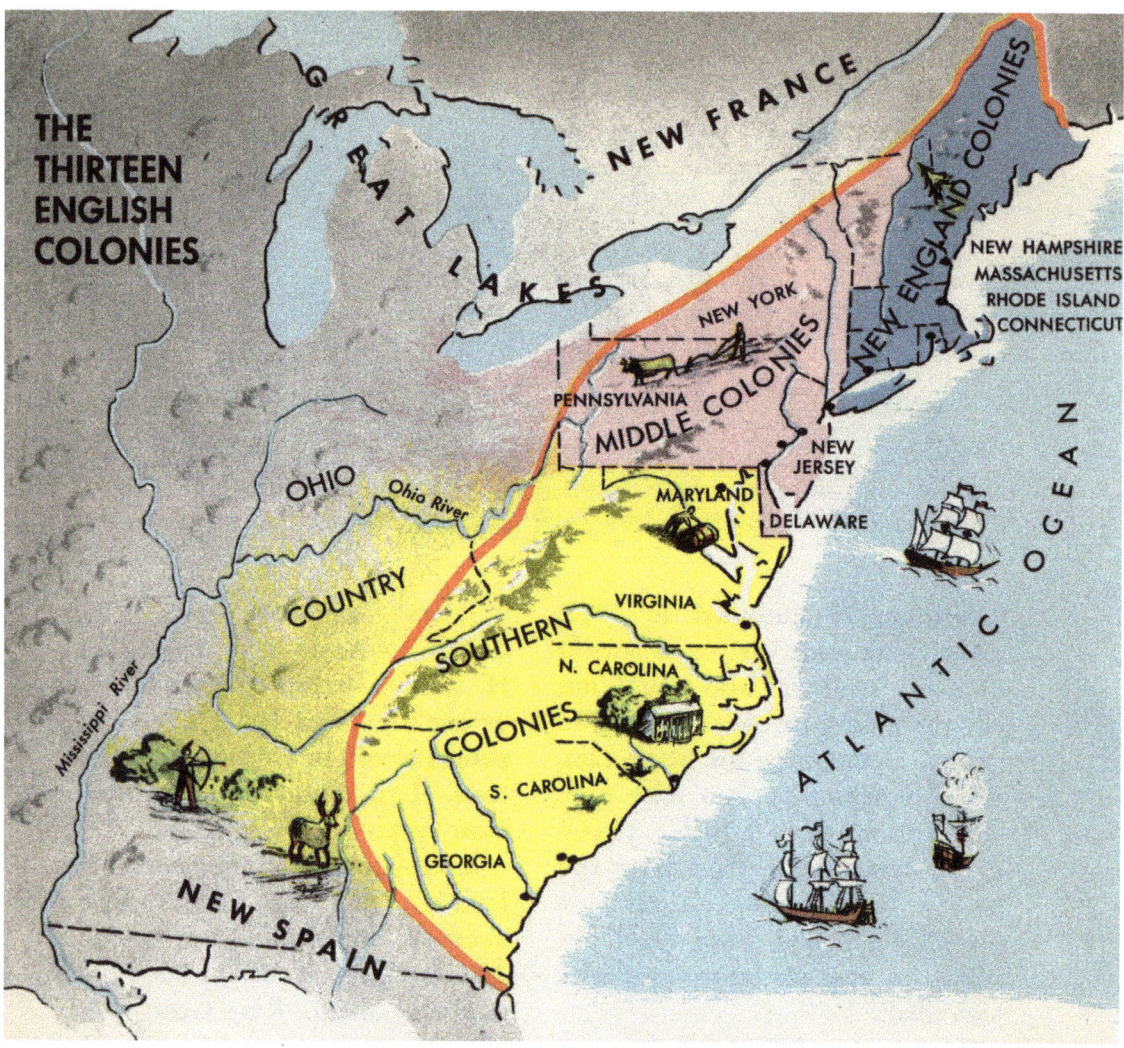

Georgia was the thirteenth, and last, English colony. It was settled 126 years after the first English settlers came to Jamestown. George Washington was already one year old when Georgia was founded. James Oglethorpe lived to see Georgia become a state instead of a colony. It was one of the thirteen original states.

We have now read how all the English colonies were founded. There were thirteen of these colonies. Four were New England Colonies. Four were Middle Colonies. Five were Southern Colonies.

On the map above you see all thirteen of the colonies. In the next chapter we shall read how the people lived in these colonies.

14. THE SOUTHERN COLONIES

STUDY LESSON

WHERE IS IT? Answer each question in a complete sentence.

1. Maryland was north of what colony?
2. Which colony was just south of Virginia?
3. Name the Southern colonies.
4. Which English colony was located between South Carolina and Florida?

WHAT AM I? Write each name and after it the phrase that explains it.

1. Maryland
2. Jamestown
3. Georgia
4. Toleration Act
5. Florida
6. Carolina

a. a law that gave Maryland's colonists freedom of religion.
b. a Spanish colony.
c. the first English settlement in North America.
d. first colony to grant freedom of religion.
e. colony started for people in debt.
f. land south of Virginia.

WHAT IS THE REASON? Think carefully before you answer each question.

1. Why was Maryland colony started?
2. Why did Oglethorpe found the colony of Georgia?
3. Why did Catholics have to suffer in Maryland in later years?
4. Why did King George allow Oglethorpe to start a colony in Georgia?

WORDS TO KNOW. Use each of these words in a sentence. Look them up in your dictionary if you are not sure of their meaning.

tobacco   debts   neighbors
chapel   prison

WHO AM I? Write each name and after it the phrase that tells about him.

1. Lord Baltimore
2. James Oglethorpe
3. Leonard Calvert
4. Father Andrew White
5. George II

a. the King of England.
b. used an Indian hut as a chapel.
c. was given land by King George.
d. brother of Lord Baltimore.
e. became a Catholic in England.

SOMETHING TO THINK ABOUT. Think carefully before you answer these questions.

1. How did Maryland show that Catholics believe in freedom of religion?
2. Do you think that it was a good idea to put people in prison because they owed money?
3. What other reason, besides kindness to debtors, did the King have for allowing James Oglethorpe to start a colony in Georgia?

15. How People Lived in the English Colonies

Living in the Middle Colonies. Farming and trading were the chief occupations. Farmers raised wheat, corn, oats, and rye. Fruit trees did well and there were good grazing lands for cows and sheep. Milk, cheese and butter, and wool and yarn were leading products.

New York and Philadelphia were both good ports, so ship owners and traders got rich. Ships carried goods back and forth from New England and the South to the Middle Colonies. Fur trade with the Indians was most profitable because the Indians traded their expensive furs for cheap beads and liquor.

You have already seen how the Dutch people lived in their part of the Middle Colonies. Now you are going to see how English settlers lived close by in another part of the Middle Colonies.

A Family in Pennsylvania. This is the Taylor family. The Taylors live on a farm in Pennsylvania. It is the year 1720.

The Taylors are all in the kitchen. The kitchen was the most important room in a colonial house. The mother cooked the meals over the big open fireplace, as you see in the picture on page 131. In cold weather the kitchen was the only warm room in the house. Everybody stayed near the fireplace and did their work near the fireplace. They ate in the kitchen. Sometimes some members of the family even slept in the kitchen.

15. How People Lived in the English Colonies

Mr. Taylor came to America from England twenty years ago, in 1700. He was a Catholic, so he settled in Pennsylvania. At that time Pennsylvania was the only English colony in which Catholics were allowed to practice their religion.

Mr. Taylor's land was covered by trees when he first saw it. He had to cut down many trees in order to make room for a house. Men from other farms helped him build his house. Then he had to cut down more trees so he could plant his crops. All this was very hard work. Mr. Taylor married after living in Pennsylvania for several years.

All the Taylor children were born on the farm in Pennsylvania. They have never been more than 20 miles from the farm. The roads are very bad, and it is not easy to travel. They have never seen a city. Sometimes, in the evenings when the work is done, Mr. Taylor tells them about the big ocean he crossed when he came to America. It is hard for the children to picture such things.

"But you should thank God that you are here in Pennsylvania," Mr. Taylor says. "When I was in England I was not allowed to practice my religion. I could not find any work to do. I was often cold and hungry. Once when I could not pay a small sum of money that I owed I was put into prison.

"Here it is different. Here, a priest comes around every month to say Mass for us. Catholics meet once a week to say prayers together.

We own this large farm. We do have to work hard, but we have a house, we have plenty of food, and we have warm clothes. Back where I come from we would not have any of these things."

Everybody Worked on a Colonial Farm. Take another look at the picture at the beginning of this chapter. You will notice that everybody is working. Men, women, and children all worked on a colonial farm. They worked from early in the morning till late at night.

The Taylors do almost everything for themselves. They raise all their own food. They make all their own clothes. They make their own furniture. They even make the candles which they need for lights. The only things they buy are their tools.

15. How People Lived in the English Colonies

Do the Taylor children go to school? The boys attend school a few months in the winter. There is not so much work to do on the farm in the winter. They learn to read and write and they learn something about numbers. They do not learn much else. The girls do not go to school at all. Their mother teaches them how to cook and sew.

Mr. and Mrs. Taylor both teach the children the truths of their Catholic faith.

Do the Taylors ever have any good times? Yes, but their good times are different from yours. They have no movies, no radio, no television. They make their own good times. The girls have homemade dolls. The boys have homemade sleds. Sometimes the neighbors gather together. They sing songs, dance, and play games.

How People in New England Lived.

We have just had a look at the Taylor family. The Taylors lived in Pennsylvania. Suppose the Taylors had lived in one of the other colonies instead of Pennsylvania. Suppose they had lived in one of the New England colonies, for example.

If the Taylors had lived in New England their lives would have been the same in some ways. In other ways their lives would have been different.

If they had lived in New England they probably would have been farmers just as they were in Pennsylvania. Nine out of ten people in all the English colonies were farmers.

In New England the farms were smaller than in Pennsylvania. The ground was not as good for raising crops and there were many stones. This meant that New England farmers had to work very hard to make a living.

Many of the people in New England lived in villages. They went out from the village every day to work in the fields. The houses in a village were often built around an open space. This space was called the village green. Anyone might bring his cows to feed on the grass of the green. The men of the village sometimes drilled here, like soldiers. Boys sometimes played marbles on the green.

Every village had a blacksmith. His chief task was to make iron shoes for the horses. He also made iron pots and kettles and many kinds of tools.

Each village also had a carpenter and a cobbler. A cobbler is a man who makes shoes.

The House.

The house was long and narrow. The door opened on a tiny hall with the living room on one side and the family bedroom on the other. There might be a small bedroom upstairs. There was no kitchen.

15. How People Lived in the English Colonies

The huge living room served for cooking and eating and working. A big fireplace gave heat and light. Mother cooked in kettles hung over the fire. She baked in a brick oven on one side. Grown-ups sat before the fire on a long, plain bench with a high back to keep out drafts. Children sat on three-legged stools in the chimney corner. Almost every living room had a spinning wheel for making thread, a loom for making cloth, and a churn for making butter.

No Freedom of Religion in New England. The Taylors could hear Mass. If they had lived in New England they probably would not have been able to hear Mass. Priests were not allowed in most of the New England colonies.

There was a Puritan Church in almost every village. The people had to go to this church or else pay a fine. For this reason, not many Catholics went to New England.

The New England colonies had more schools than the other colonies. Everyone had to pay a tax to support the schools, just as our public schools are supported today. The Puritan religion was taught in these schools, along with reading, writing, and arithmetic.

The people of New England did not have half as much fun as the people of other colonies. The Puritans did not allow card playing, dancing, and many other kinds of amusements. They thought these things were sinful.

The People of New England Turn to the Sea. If the Taylors had lived in New England their father might not have been a farmer. He might have been a sailor or a fisherman, a lumberman or a rum trader.

Because the land was so poor, all the people of New England could not make their living by farming. There were many big trees in the forest. Some men became lumbermen. They cut down the trees and sawed them into boards. Some of the lumber was used in New England. Some of it was sent to Europe. Some New England men became shipbuilders. Some who lived near the ocean became sailors and fishermen.

Many of the richest people of New England made their money by trading with the islands in the West Indies. New England ships sailed to the Dutch and Spanish islands with cargoes of fish, lumber, flour, and wheat. The traders sold their goods and bought sugar and molasses. New Englanders used the molasses to make rum, a favorite drink in the colonies.

Some of the rum was shipped from New England to Africa and exchanged for slaves. The slaves were brought to the West Indies and exchanged for more molasses. The molasses was then brought to New England to make more rum.

The New Englanders made money on each sale. The rum makers, ship owners, and slave traders were getting rich. Later on, when England tried to stop this trade, these wealthy shippers were ready to rebel. This was one of the causes of the American Revolution.

How the Colonies Were Governed. John Adams belongs to the Massachusetts Colony. We ask him how the colony is governed. He tells us that the assembly makes most of the laws.

"There is also a Parliament in England," John says. "This Parliament makes laws for England and all the lands ruled by England. So we have to obey Parliament as well as our assembly. Parliament can also set aside laws which were passed by our assembly. It has not done this very often. I am afraid there would be trouble if Parliament set aside many laws passed by our assembly. I hope that will never happen."

John also tells us that Massachusetts has a governor who is appointed by the King of England. This governor does not have as much power as the governor of New France or the viceroy of New Spain.

"The assembly pays the governor's salary," John tells us. "And we elect the members of the assembly. If the governor does something we do not like we can stop paying his salary. No governor wants this to happen."

We ask John if the government is the same in each of the thirteen English colonies.

"There are small differences," he says. "But in most ways the governments are alike. Each colony has a governor and each colony has an assembly. And, of course, each colony is under the Parliament in England."

We ask John if all the people of Massachusetts have the right to vote.

"No," he says. "Women are not allowed to vote. Nor are all the men. Usually only men who own a certain amount of property are allowed to vote in any of the English colonies except Pennsylvania."

We can see that even the people in the English colonies did not have complete self-government. This was because so few people were allowed to vote. But the colonists were very proud of what self-government they did have. The people in the French and Spanish lands had no self-government at all.

Later American colonists thought England was trying to take away their self-government. This frightened them very much. The American colonists always loved their freedom. We shall see how the fear of losing their freedom made the colonists break away from England. This is how our country, the United States of America, began.

How People Lived in the Southern Colonies. In the Southern Colonies there were large farms which were called plantations. Usually, one large crop was raised on each plantation. Tobacco was raised on some plantations. Rice was raised on others. Indigo was raised on others. Indigo is a plant from which blue dye can be made.

Tobacco, rice, and indigo were not grown to be used by the planters. They were raised to be sold. Such crops are called staple crops or money crops. Tobacco was the money crop grown in the South for many, many years. Later cotton became the money crop. These money crops made the owners of the plantation or planters wealthy.

Most of the plantations were near a river. Each plantation had a wharf. Ocean vessels came up to the wharfs. The ships sailed off to England loaded with tobacco, or rice, or indigo. They came back with clothes, books, and furniture which the plantation owners had ordered from England. The plantation owners never lost touch with England. They did not have to make everything for themselves as did the Taylors and most other farmers of New England and the Middle Colonies.

15. How People Lived in the English Colonies

The wealthy Southern planters could afford to build beautiful homes. These houses were made of brick, stone, and timber. The woodwork inside was of the finest woods often brought from Europe. Outside, the houses were decorated with broad columns and usually painted white.

These houses had many rooms for the family and their guests. Since the plantations were so large, the only neighbors were far, far away. Visiting became the custom. Southern families took great pride in making their guests feel at home. Southerners became known for their hospitality. The friendly welcome shown to guests is called hospitality.

Travel from plantation to plantation was not easy. Many of the plantations were located on rivers. These could be reached by boats—a common means of transportation in those days. Many years later roads were made. Then travel by horse and carriage became possible. Horse-drawn carriages which traveled over a regular route were called stagecoaches. The distance between two stops on a trip was called a stage.

The planters needed a great deal of help. Negro slaves did most of the work on the plantations. These slaves belonged to the plantation owners. They were not paid for their work. They were given a place to live, and food, and clothes, but that was about all. They were not allowed to run away. Slaves were bought and sold like animals.

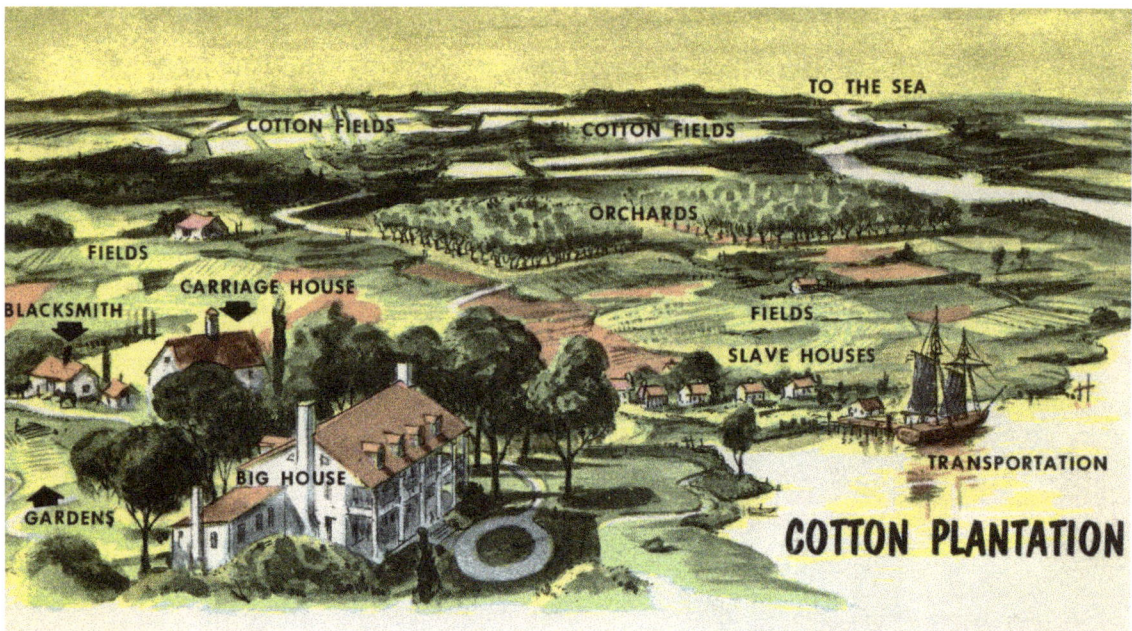

Every plantation had its own garden patch. Here corn, wheat, and vegetables such as potatoes, carrots, turnips, and parsnips were grown. Pear trees and apple trees provided fresh fruit. These crops were not for sale. They were for the planter and his family and slaves to eat.

Each plantation had its own carpenters and blacksmiths. There were few schools in the South. Many plantation owners hired teachers, or tutors, for the children. Some of the boys were sent to England to go to school.

Not all the farmers of the South lived on large plantations. Far back from the rivers and the ocean were many small farms. The people who lived on these farms did not have any slaves. They had to work very hard for a living.

Most of the children who lived on these small farms did not go to school. The children of the slaves did not go to school either.

The Southern plantation owners had many ways of having a good time. They loved horse racing and hunting, dancing and card playing.

If the Taylors had lived in the Southern Colonies they would not have been allowed to practice their religion. Everyone had to belong to the Church of England in these colonies. Maryland, as we know, was started for the Catholics. But even in Maryland, after 1689, Catholics were punished for practicing their religion.

15. How People Lived in the English Colonies

STUDY LESSON

WHERE IS IT? Answer each question in a complete sentence.

1. Name the English colonies.
2. Along what coast of America are the English colonies?
3. Is Pennsylvania a New England, a Middle, or a Southern colony?
4. In what colonies were plantations found?
5. In what colonies was farming most difficult?

WHAT AM I? Write each word and after it the phrase that explains it.

1. plantation   2. cobbler   3. village
4. indigo   5. slaves   6. tobacco

a. a man who makes shoes.
b. a plant from which blue dye is made.
c. a crop raised on Southern plantations.
d. a very large farm in the Southern colonies.
e. a place where houses are built close together.
f. Negroes who worked on large Southern plantations.

WORDS TO KNOW. Use each of these words in a sentence. Look them up in your dictionary if you are not sure of their meaning.

plow   dye   wharf
tax   tutors   mansion

WHAT IS THE REASON? Think carefully before you answer each question.

1. Why did Mr. Taylor come to Pennsylvania instead of coming to one of the other English colonies?
2. Why was the Taylor family better off on a farm in Pennsylvania than they would have been in Europe?
3. Why did New England farmers have to work very hard to make a living?
4. Why did plantation owners in the Southern Colonies have slaves?
5. Why did the people of other colonies have better times than the people from New England?

SOMETHING TO THINK ABOUT. Think carefully before you answer these questions.

1. Are Catholics now allowed to practice their religion everywhere in the United States? Do you know if they are allowed to practice their religion everywhere in the world today?
2. Why should Catholics love their country?
3. Imagine! In Pennsylvania there were so few priests that Mass could be heard only once a month. How many times a day is Mass said in your parish?

  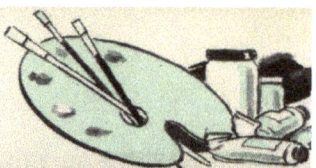

SCRAPBOOK OF FAMOUS PEOPLE

ADD THESE STORIES TO YOUR SCRAPBOOK WITH PICTURES OR DRAWINGS OF THE MEN.

PETER STUYVESANT FORCED THE SETTLERS TO BELONG TO THE DUTCH REFORMED CHURCH AND REFUSED TO LET THE SETTLERS HAVE A VOICE IN THE GOVERNMENT. IF YOU WERE A DUTCH SETTLER WOULD YOU HAVE FOUGHT FOR STUYVESANT OR SURRENDERED TO THE ENGLISH? WRITE A LITTLE STORY ABOUT THE DUTCH GOVERNOR.

IF THE KING OWED YOU SOME MONEY WOULD YOU HAVE TAKEN INSTEAD A PIECE OF LAND IN THE WILDERNESS WHERE PEOPLE COULD PRACTICE THEIR OWN RELIGION? WILLIAM PENN DID. WRITE A STORY TELLING ABOUT PENN.

JAMES OGLETHORPE FELT SORRY FOR THE PEOPLE HE SAW BEING KEPT IN PRISON BECAUSE THEY WERE TOO POOR TO PAY THEIR DEBTS. WRITE A STORY ABOUT HIM SHOWING THE KIND OF PERSON HE WAS.

THINGS FROM LONG AGO

1. MAKE A MODEL OF THE FAMOUS PILGRIM SHIP, THE *MAYFLOWER*.
2. MAKE A CHART LISTING THE COLONIES YOU HAVE READ ABOUT.
   a. WRITE THE DATE OF THE FOUNDING OF EACH OF THESE COLONIES.
   b. WRITE THE NAME OF THE LEADER OF THE COLONY.
   c. WRITE THE LOCATION OF EACH COLONY: NEW ENGLAND, MIDDLE, OR SOUTHERN.
3. USING CARDBOARD OR PAPER, MAKE
   a) A PILGRIM HAT.
   b) A THREE-CORNERED HAT LIKE THOSE WORN IN THE SOUTH.

15. How People Lived in the English Colonies

BOOKS

PLAYS

THIS IS HOW IT HAPPENED

PLAN A PLAY CALLED "QUIET CONQUEST"

SCENE I: PETER STUYVESANT GIVES ORDERS TO THE DUTCH SETTLERS.

SCENE II: PETER STUYVESANT RECEIVES THE NOTE FROM THE ENGLISH AND TEARS IT UP. THE DUTCH READ THE TORN NOTE AND TALK ABOUT SURRENDER.

SCENE III: THE ENGLISH ARRIVE AND TAKE COMMAND. THE PLACE IS NAMED NEW YORK.

SEEING AMERICA

DRAW OR TRACE A MAP OF THE ATLANTIC COAST OF NORTH AMERICA AND MARK THE LOCATION OF THE THIRTEEN COLONIES. COLOR THE NEW ENGLAND COLONIES GREEN, THE MIDDLE COLONIES RED, AND THE SOUTHERN COLONIES BLUE.

NAME GAME

USING THE NAMES OF PERSONS WHO HAVE APPEARED IN UNIT THREE, PLAY THE GAME WHICH WAS DESCRIBED AT THE END OF UNIT ONE.

COLONIAL INFORMATION CENTER

IF YOU HAD LIVED DURING COLONIAL TIMES, LIFE WOULD HAVE BEEN VERY DIFFERENT FOR YOU. WHAT GAMES WOULD YOU HAVE PLAYED? HOW WOULD YOU HAVE LIKED SCHOOL THEN? IN A LIBRARY YOU WILL FIND MANY BOOKS ON THE LIVES OF COLONIAL CHILDREN. HERE ARE A FEW YOU MIGHT LOOK FOR.

Author	Title	Publisher
DE ANGELI	ELIN'S AMERIKA	DOUBLEDAY
	JARED'S ISLAND	DOUBLEDAY
	SKIPPACK SCHOOL	DOUBLEDAY
HUMPHREY	HOW NEW ENGLAND WAS MADE	LOTHROP, LEE & SHEPARD
MALOY AND DALGLIESH	WOODEN SHOES IN AMERICA	SCRIBNER
PERKINS	THE PURITAN TWINS	HOUGHTON MIFFLIN
	PILGRIM STORIES AND PLAYS	RAND McNALLY
STONE AND FICKETT	EVERYDAY LIFE IN THE COLONIES	HEATH

LOOKING INTO THE LONG AGO

"Now, if you will turn off the lights," said Mr. North, "I will show the movies."

"I took these pictures at our Fourth of July picnic," Mr. North said, "but I have never seen them myself. I do not own a projector. When I heard the Davis family was coming, I borrowed a projector."

"I can hardly wait to see the pictures," said Mary Jean.

Mr. North clicked the switch on the projector. The screen lighted up. In a moment, the North and Davis families were watching their Fourth of July picnic.

"Oh look," Mary said. "Dick and I are playing 'last tag'. I didn't know you took pictures of that, Uncle Tom. Look! There I go over the brook. I am crossing on the stones. I made it! Now here comes Dick after me."

"Oh, oh," Dick groaned. He knew what was going to happen next.

The movies showed Dick stepping from stone to stone. When he got to the middle of the brook, his foot slipped. He went into the water with a splash.

Everyone in the room laughed at the picture of Dick sitting in the water.

Suddenly the picture on the screen changed. There was no longer a picture of Dick sitting in the water. Now there was a picture of a man's head.

"Who is that?" asked Dick.

"That's a man who lived a long time ago," said Mary Jean. "You can tell by his clothes and by the way he wears his hair."

"What is he doing in our Fourth of July pictures?" Dick asked.

Mr. North turned off the projector. Dick turned on the lights.

Mr. North was laughing when the lights came on.

"After the picnic I had a little film left in the camera," he said. "I wanted to use it up. I also wanted to see whether I could photograph a picture from a book. I found this picture of Thomas Jefferson in one of my books. It turned out well, didn't it?"

"Yes," Dick said, "but I do not like having Thomas Jefferson on our Fourth of July film."

"I can cut him off if you want me to," said Mr. North. "But you should not mind having Thomas Jefferson on a Fourth of July film. What is the Fourth of July?"

"It is our country's birthday."

"That is right. The people who lived in the English colonies did not like the way England was treating them. These people elected some men to a Congress. The members of Congress signed a Declaration of Independence. They adopted it on July 4, 1776."

Mr. North was now putting the projector back into the case.

"Do you know who wrote the Declaration of Independence?" he asked.

"I'll bet I can guess," said Mary Jean. "Was it Thomas Jefferson?"

"Yes," said Mr. North. "Some day you will learn part of the Declaration of Independence. You will learn the part which says that all men are created equal. You will learn the part which says that all men have certain rights which cannot be taken away. Those are important words, and you will understand them better when you are a little older. It was Thomas Jefferson who wrote those words."

"Well," said Dick, "I guess you will not have to cut Thomas Jefferson off the Fourth of July film. He really belongs there." Then Dick remembered the picture of himself falling into the brook. "In fact," he said, "I wish there were more of Jefferson and less of me."

16. The French Lose Their Land in North America

Washington Carries a Message. The young man in this picture is George Washington. He is 21 years old. It is the year 1753. The governor of Virginia has sent George Washington on a very important errand.

What is the errand? We shall understand it better if we look at the map.

The thirteen English colonies, as you see, were along the shores of the Atlantic Ocean. The people who lived in the colonies were called colonists. Very few of the colonists crossed the Appalachian Mountains at first. By 1750 some of the colonists were thinking about crossing the mountains. They wished to build homes and start farms near the Ohio River. You can see the Ohio River on the map.

The colonists were sure that the Ohio Valley belonged to them. John Cabot had claimed all of North America for the English.

But the French were also sure that the Ohio Valley belonged to them. La Salle had stood at the mouth of the Mississippi River and had claimed all the land drained by that river.

"The Ohio River empties into the Mississippi River," the French said. "Therefore, the Ohio country belongs to us."

The French began building forts in the Ohio country. They did this so they could keep soldiers there. The soldiers would keep the English settlers from moving into the rich Ohio country.

16. The French Lose Their Land in North America

The governor of Virginia was angry when he learned what the French were doing. He wanted to tell them to stop building forts. Who could he send with the important message? He selected George Washington, who was then a major in the army.

That is why we see George Washington crossing the mountains in the winter of 1753. He is carrying an important message from the governor of Virginia to the commander of the French soldiers in the Ohio country.

The message says that the Ohio country belongs to the English. The message asks the French to stop building forts there.

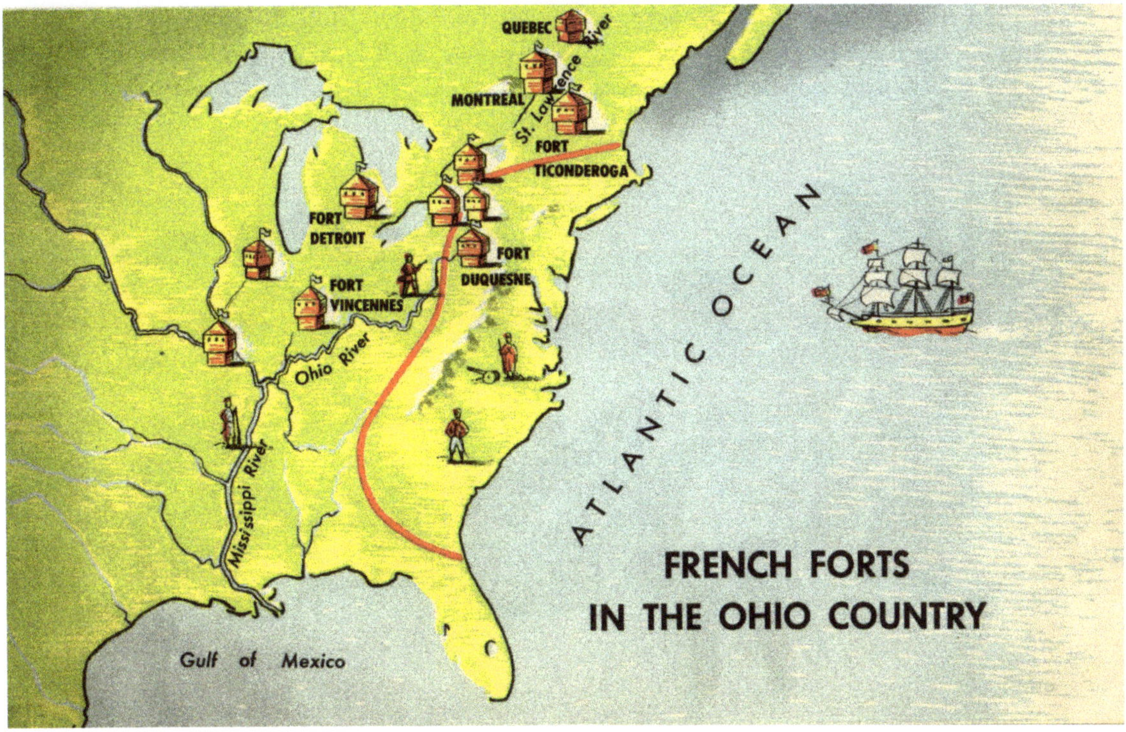

FRENCH FORTS IN THE OHIO COUNTRY

How the French and Indian War Began. Major Washington delivered his message. The French general told Washington that the French would not leave the Ohio Valley.

Washington had a long, dangerous trip back to Virginia. Indians shot arrows at him and his men. He nearly lost his life when his raft turned over in an icy stream. He and his men had to sleep on the frozen ground with no tents over them. At last Washington reached Virginia. He told the governor that the French would not stop building forts.

In 1754 the governor sent Washington back to the Ohio country with some soldiers. Washington's small army was surrounded by French and Indians. Washington was forced to surrender, and so he returned to Virginia.

The French and Indian War had begun. The English called it the French and Indian War, because they had to fight both French soldiers and Indian warriors. Most of the Indians were on

16. The French Lose Their Land in North America

the side of the French. The Iroquois Indians, however, were on the side of the English. The Iroquois had been enemies of the French ever since the days of Champlain.

The King of England sent General Edward Braddock to take charge of the English Army in America. General Braddock decided to capture Fort Duquesne. The French had built this important fort at the place where two rivers join to form the Ohio River.

General Braddock had done much fighting in Europe. Most of this fighting was done on open fields. He did not know very much about fighting in the forests of North America. Braddock had his men march as if they were in a parade. Their flags waved in the breeze. The French and Indians shot at them from behind trees and stones. The British soldiers wore bright red coats. These made good targets for the French and Indians. Many of Braddock's men were killed. Braddock himself was wounded and later died from the wounds. After General Braddock was wounded, George Washington took charge of the army. He saved what was left of it.

The War Ends. For every Frenchman in North America there were about 18 English colonists. You would think that it would have been easy for the English to defeat the French. But the French defeated General Braddock, as we have just seen. The French continued to win most of the battles for the next two years.

How could the French win so many battles when there were so many more Englishmen? There were a number of reasons. For one thing, the French had a larger army in North America than the English had. The French had the help of many Indians. The French were also united under one government. The English had thirteen colonies, and at first the colonies did not work together very well.

In 1757, the government in England began to take more interest in the war in America. A man named William Pitt was put in charge of the war. Pitt sent more soldiers to America. He also sent some good generals. One of these generals was James Wolfe.

After 1757, the English began to win most of the battles. The English captured Fort Duquesne in 1758. George Washington fought with the army that captured Fort Duquesne. The name of the fort was changed to Fort Pitt, after

William Pitt. The city that stands on this spot today is named Pittsburgh.

The English captured one fort after another, but the French still held Quebec, the capital of New France. General Wolfe decided to capture Quebec. The task seemed impossible. Quebec was a powerful fort on a high cliff above the St. Lawrence River. The French in the fort would shoot at anybody who tried to climb the cliff. The fort was in command of a brave leader, General Montcalm, one of the best generals the French had.

16. The French Lose Their Land in North America

General Wolfe had his ships sail past Quebec in the dead of night. There were no lights on the ships, so the French did not see them sailing by. When they had passed the fort, General Wolfe had his men get off the ships. He had them climb the cliff. It was a hard, dangerous climb. The men had to cling to bushes and rocks. They had to be very quiet, so the French soldiers in the fort would not hear them.

In the morning the French were surprised to find the British army just outside their fort. There was a bitter battle, but it did not last long. The British captured the fort. Both General Wolfe and General Montcalm were killed in the battle.

Quebec was captured in September, 1759. This ended the fighting in North America. The French and English were still fighting in other parts of the world, however. Finally, the French were defeated everywhere.

The peace treaty was signed in Paris in 1763.

16. The French Lose Their Land in North America

The End of the French Power in North America. When the peace treaty was signed France was forced to give up almost all her land in North America. The map shows how North America was divided by the Treaty of Paris.

1. England took Canada from France.

2. England took from France all the land east of the Mississippi River except the city of New Orleans.

3. Spain had helped France in the war, so England took Florida from Spain.

4. To pay Spain for losing Florida, France gave Spain the territory between the Mississippi River and the Rocky Mountains. France also gave Spain the city of New Orleans.

5. France was allowed to keep a few small islands near the Gulf of St. Lawrence. French fishermen used these islands for drying their fish.

France once had a great empire in North America. Now France had only a few small islands.

England once had only the thirteen colonies and some land around Hudson Bay. Now England owned almost half the continent.

The War and the Colonists. The French and Indian War had many effects upon the English colonists:

1. The colonists had always been afraid of the French. They thought that they needed the English soldiers to protect them from the French. Now the French were gone. The colonists did not think that they needed the English soldiers any longer.

2. The colonists had learned to fight as well as the English soldiers. Later, they would not be afraid to fight the English.

3. The colonists learned that war is expensive. Paying for the war caused trouble between the colonies and England.

4. The war showed the colonies that they must work together. Before the war the colonies had little to do with each other. They were jealous of one another. They had to unite to fight the French. Later, they would unite to fight the English.

In 1763, England was proud and happy. She had won a large amount of territory in North America. Within 20 years, however, she was to lose much of this territory and she was to lose most of her colonists.

A new nation was to arise in North America—the United States of America.

JEAN, A FRENCH COLONIST

Jean is a colonist in New France. His father decided to go to Canada. He wanted to make his fortune in the fur trade. He settled in Canada near the St. Lawrence River.

Like all the French colonists they are Catholics. They are farmers. They live in a little cabin on an estate owned by a lord. For the use of the land Jean must pay a small yearly rent and do some work for the lord. Farmers like Jean cannot own their own land.

If Jean or his family are sick, they will be taken to the Catholic hospital in Montreal. It is run by the Sisters. His children may go to a school and be taught by the Ursuline Sisters. They came to Quebec in 1639 to serve the Indians and white people.

Jean takes no part in making the laws of New France and he cannot vote. The colony is ruled by a governor and another man chosen by the King of France. The third leading man in the colony is the Bishop.

After the English defeated the French and Indians in a war, this part of New France was given to the English. Then many English settlers came to live in Canada. Jean and his French neighbors continued to live in peace with the new English settlers.

16. The French Lose Their Land in North America

STUDY LESSON

WHO AM I? Write the name of each person listed. Next to it write the sentence which tells you about the person.

1. George Washington
2. La Salle
3. Edward Braddock
4. John Cabot
5. General Wolfe
6. General Montcalm

a. I laid claim to all of North America for the English.
b. I was at the head of the English army at Quebec.
c. I was sent by the Governor of Virginia to carry a message to the French in the Ohio Valley.
d. I led the French army at Quebec.
e. I claimed all the land drained by the Mississippi River for France.
f. I was used to fighting in Europe and did not know how to fight in America.

WHAT AM I? Write each name and after it the phrase that explains it.

1. Iroquois 2. Quebec 3. Florida 4. Fort Duquesne 5. New Orleans

a. captured by the English in 1758.
b. city given to Spain at the end of the French and Indian War.
c. the Indians who were on the side of the English
d. given by Spain to England.
e. the capital of New France.

SOMETHING TO THINK ABOUT. Think carefully before you answer these questions.

1. How did the French and Indian War unite the Thirteen Colonies?
2. Why did the French win most of the battles at the beginning of the French and Indian War, even though there were more English people?
3. Why was General Braddock and his army defeated by the French and Indians?
4. Why did England begin winning the French and Indian war after 1757?
5. Why was the name of Fort Duquesne changed to Fort Pitt?

DATES TO REMEMBER. Write each date in column A. Next write the phrase in column B that matches the date.

A	B
1. 1763	a. capture of Quebec.
2. 1758	b. English captured Fort Duquesne.
3. 1759	c. Treaty of Paris.

WORDS TO KNOW. Write a sentence using each of these words. Look them up in your dictionary if you are not sure of the meaning.

drained   empire   unite
treaty   continent

17. The Colonists Declare their Freedom

Trouble With England. There was great excitement in the colonies in 1765, as these pictures show.

What were the people excited about?

After the French and Indian War, England needed money to pay for the war. Parliament makes the laws for England. The members of Parliament, therefore, had to find ways to get the money. The members of Parliament thought that some of the money should come from the colonists. They passed a law called the Stamp Act. This law said that the colonists had to place stamps on all important papers.

The storekeeper had to stamp his bills. The banker had to stamp his checks. Newspapers and pamphlets had to be stamped. So did deeds, wills, and leases. Some of the stamps cost a few cents. Others cost several dollars.

The colonists were very angry about the Stamp Act. People talked about the Stamp Act when they met on the street. Men made speeches against it. Newspaper articles and pamphlets said the tax was unfair. People paraded through the streets carrying signs saying that the Stamp Act was unfair. Some people even attacked the homes of the tax collectors.

We read in Chapter 9 that each colony had an assembly. The colonists were proud of their assemblies.

17. The Colonists Declare their Freedom

They were happy that they elected the men who made their laws and voted their taxes. Now they thought that the English Parliament was trying to change that. They thought that Parliament was trying to take away some of the powers of their assemblies. The American colonists did not like this.

The colonists did not mind paying taxes for the war, but they thought the tax laws should be passed by their own assemblies.

In the first picture at the beginning of this chapter, we see some colonists talking about the Stamp Act. If we could listen to these men, we would probably hear something like this:

"It is all right for Parliament to tax the people in England," says one man. "The people of England elect the members of Parliament. But we do not elect any members to Parliament. Therefore, Parliament has no right to tax us."

"Parliament is in London, 4000 miles away," says another man. "The members of Parliament know nothing about us or our problems."

"Our colony has its own assembly," says a third man. "We elected the members of this assembly. The assembly should make our laws and vote our taxes."

"Parliament has been unfair to us again and again," a fourth man says. "This is another unjust law."

The Stamp Tax Is Removed. Men from nine colonies held a meeting. This was called the Stamp Act Congress. The members of this Congress sent a letter to Parliament. The letter said that Parliament had no right to tax the colonists.

The Stamp Act Congress showed that men from the different colonies could work together.

The colonists agreed to stop buying goods from Great Britain. English merchants lost much money when the colonists stopped buying from them. These merchants begged Parliament to cancel the Stamp Act. Parliament did so in 1766.

Parliament insisted, however, that it still had the right to tax the colonists.

King George III. George III was the king of England at that time. He was a very stubborn man. He wished to show the colonists that they had to do what his government told them to do. The king of England did not have very much power of his own. He could not make any laws. But there were many men in Parliament who felt the same way the king did. They were called the "King's Friends." These men passed the Stamp Act and the other laws that the colonists did not like.

King George III was unhappy when Parliament canceled the Stamp Act. He was glad that Parliament at least said it

17. The Colonists Declare their Freedom

still had the right to tax the colonists any time it wished.

New Taxes Bring More Trouble. In 1767 Parliament put new taxes on paper, glass, tea, and other articles which the colonists bought from the English. King George III was happy about the new taxes. The colonists became angry once more. They were even more angry when officers were sent from England to see that the taxes were paid. These officers were even allowed to search people's homes.

The people of Boston were especially angry. The English were afraid that trouble would break out there. They sent soldiers to Boston to keep the people quiet and to protect the tax collectors. This only caused more trouble. It made the people furious to see the soldiers.

One winter night some men and boys threw snowballs at one of the soldiers. He called for help. More soldiers came. More colonists came, too. The colonists jeered at the soldiers and threw more snowballs. Then they hit the soldiers with sticks. The soldiers fired their guns. Five persons were killed and several were wounded. This was called the "Boston Massacre."

The news of this "Boston Massacre" spread through the colonies. The colonists became more excited than ever. The royal governor of Massachusetts was afraid there would be more trouble in Boston. He took the soldiers out of the city.

It is hard to say what might have happened if Parliament had refused to remove most of the new taxes about that time. The colonists were happy about this, and they forgot their anger for a while.

Just one tax was left. That was the tax on tea. King George III said: "We must keep a tax on something to show that we have a right to tax the colonies."

The Boston Tea Party. The tax on tea was to lead to even more serious trouble in the colonies. The year was 1773.

King George III thought he would trick the colonists into paying the tax on tea. Ships loaded with tea were sent to several ports in the colonies. The price of this tea was very low. The colonists would have to pay a tax, but they would be paying less for the tea than they usually paid. The king and his helpers thought that the colonists would be so glad to get cheap tea that they would not object to paying the tax.

But the colonists would not be tricked. They said that Parliament had no right to tax them. They would not allow the tea to be landed. At most ports the ships turned around and sailed back to England.

At Boston the royal governor would not let the ships sail back to England. He said that the king's order must be obeyed; the tea must be unloaded.

The colonists were also determined. They said the tea would not be unloaded. One night a group of colonists, disguised as Indians, climbed aboard the ships. They broke open the tea chests with hatchets and threw them into the water. This became known as the Boston Tea Party. It was another step toward war with England.

Many of the colonists thought that this was going too far. "It is true that England has been unjust to us," they said. "But that does not give us the right to destroy property that belongs to another."

Boston Is Punished. King George and other leaders of the English government were angry when they heard about the Boston Tea Party. They said that Boston must be punished. Parliament ordered that no ships were allowed to sail in or out of Boston harbor. The people of Boston received most of their food by ship. This meant that they would not have enough to eat. Many men of Boston made their living as merchants or sailors. Now these men were out of work.

The king sent a new governor to Massachusetts to see that his orders were carried out. The new governor was General Thomas Gage. General Gage had 5,000 soldiers. The soldiers were to see that orders were obeyed.

People in the other colonies were alarmed when they learned what had happened to Boston. They sent wagonloads of food and other supplies into the city. They also called a meeting to see what they could do.

The First Continental Congress. This meeting began in Philadelphia on September 5, 1774. Men from every colony except Georgia were there. The meeting was called the First Continental Congress. Some of the leaders who were at the meeting were Samuel Adams, Patrick Henry, John Adams, George Washington, and Benjamin Franklin.

These men drew up a list of the things the colonists were complaining about. The list was sent to England. The Congress also agreed that the colonists would not buy anything from England or sell anything to England.

This meeting showed once more that the men from the different colonies could work together. The men at this meeting voted to hold a Second Continental Congress in May, 1775. The trouble with England was becoming more serious.

Until this time the colonists thought of themselves not as Americans but as Virginians or New Yorkers or New Englanders. Patrick Henry knew it was important for the colonists to stand together in their fight with England. During the meeting of the First Continental Congress, Henry said these wise words:

"The distinctions between Virginians, and Pennsylvanians, New Yorkers and New Englanders are no more. I am not a Virginian, but an American."

The Battles of Lexington and Concord. The colonists of Massachusetts got together supplies of guns, powder, and shot. These supplies were hidden in the little town of Concord. Men drilled secretly as soldiers. These men were called "Minute Men" because they were supposed to be ready to fight at a minute's notice.

17. The Colonists Declare their Freedom

General Gage found out that the colonists had ammunition at Concord. On April 18, 1775, he sent a thousand soldiers to capture this ammunition. Paul Revere and William Dawes rode through the night to awaken the Minute Men from their sleep. When the English soldiers reached the town of Lexington the next morning a small group of Minute Men were waiting for them. Shots were fired. Eight Minute Men were killed.

The English marched on to Concord. More Minute Men were waiting. There was another battle. The soldiers destroyed all the ammunition they could find. Then they marched back to Boston. On the way back the colonists fired at them from behind every stone and every tree. More than one-fourth of the English soldiers were killed before they reached Boston.

The Battle of Bunker Hill. The Minute Men dug trenches on one of the hills near Boston. On June 17, 1775, General Gage ordered his men to attack the colonists. Three thousand English soldiers charged up the hill. Not a gun was fired until they came within a few yards of the American line. Then came a killing fire from the Americans.

The English fell back, and charged a second time. The same thing happened again. By this time the Americans were almost out of ammunition. The English took the hill when they charged the third time. This was called the Battle of Bunker Hill. The English won the Battle of Bunker Hill because they had more men and more ammunition. But the colonists had showed that they were good fighters.

The Declaration of Independence. The Second Continental Congress met in Philadelphia, in May, 1775. When the Congress first met, the members did not think of breaking away from England. They said that they were loyal to the King.

17. The Colonists Declare their Freedom

They said that they were only asking for fair treatment.

As time went on, they saw that they could not expect fair treatment from the King or from the "King's Friends" in Parliament. They finally decided that there was only one thing to do. They must break away from England now if ever they wished to be free.

Congress asked Thomas Jefferson and some other men to write a Declaration of Independence. Jefferson did almost all the writing. He said that the United States of America was now a free country and no longer belonged to England.

The members of Congress read the Declaration of Independence which Jefferson had written. On July 4, 1776, they voted to adopt it.

July 4 is the birthday of the United States. On that day, in 1776, the United States of America was born.

JOHN, THE MINUTE MAN

John was a farmer who lived in Massachusetts. John was afraid that the English were trying to take away the liberty and the self-government of the colonists.

"Some day," John said to his wife, "we colonists may have to fight to protect our liberty. We should be ready to fight when that time comes."

So John joined the Minute Men. Two or three times a week he left his farm and went to the village. There he met with other Minute Men. They elected leaders. They planned what they would do if the time came when they must fight.

At his farm, John kept a gun and powder and shot. He had to be ready to fight at a minute's notice. That is why he was called a Minute Man.

One day John rode to the town of Concord with a load of hay. He passed some English soldiers. They looked at his wagon full of hay, but they did not stop him. The soldiers did not know that he had powder and shot hidden under the hay. At Concord, John put the powder and shot in a secret hiding place. Other Minute Men also brought powder and shot to Concord.

One night there was a loud knocking at the door of John's farm house. It was just after midnight on April 19, 1775. He put his head out the bedroom window. The man at the door was another Minute Man. "Hurry John," the man cried. "English soldiers are on the way to Lexington and Concord. At Concord they will try to capture the powder and shot which we have hidden. Other Minute Men are going to Lexington. We are to go to Concord."

Then the man rode quickly off to tell the news to another Minute Man.

John dressed in a hurry and grabbed his gun. He said goodbye to his wife. He kissed his children as they slept. In a minute he was on his horse and racing toward Concord.

Shots were fired at Lexington and Concord. Men were killed. This was the beginning of a long war between the colonists and the English. The war lasted six years. At the end of the war the colonies no longer belonged to England. They were free. They were the United States of America. Minute Men like John had helped to win this freedom.

17. The Colonists Declare their Freedom

STUDY LESSON

WHO AM I? Write the name of each person listed. Next to it write the sentence which tells you about the person.

1. King George III 2. Paul Revere
3. Samuel Adams 4. General Gage
5. Thomas Jefferson

a. I wrote the Declaration of Independence.
b. I rode to warn the Minute Men that the British were coming.
c. I ordered my men to attack the colonists at Bunker Hill.
d. I wanted to tax the colonists to help pay for the French and Indian War.
e. I was at the meeting of the First Continental Congress.

WHAT AM I? Write each name and after it the phrase that explains it.

1. Parliament
2. Boston Tea Party
3. Declaration of Independence
4. Stamp Act
5. First Continental Congress
6. Boston Massacre

a. law that placed a tax on papers.
b. said the colonies were free.
c. makes laws for England.
d. meeting of men from every American colony except Georgia.
e. when English soldiers killed five colonists.
f. American colonists in disguise as Indians.

SOMETHING TO THINK ABOUT. Think carefully before you answer these questions.

1. Do you think the colonists had the right to dump the tea into Boston Harbor?
2. Why was it wrong for the British to close Boston Harbor?
3. Why did the English Parliament cancel the Stamp Act in 1766?
4. Why were the British able to win the Battle of Bunker Hill?
5. Why did King George III and Parliament want to keep the tax on tea?
6. Why did the colonists feel that Parliament had no right to tax them?

DATES TO REMEMBER. Write each date in column A. Next write the phrase in column B it matches.

	A	B
1.	1776	a. Battle of Bunker Hill.
2.	1774	b. Signing of the Declaration of Independence.
3.	1775	c. First Continental Congress.

WORDS TO KNOW. Write a sentence using each of these words. Look them up in your dictionary if you are not sure of the meaning.

lease   will   assembly

ammunition   independence

18. Americans Win Their Freedom

George Washington Becomes Commander-in-Chief. "The English soldiers must be driven out of Boston," said the members of the Second Continental Congress.

In the last chapter we read that General Gage had 5,000 English soldiers in Boston. He would not allow ships to come in or out of Boston Harbor. His soldiers had fought the Minute Men at Lexington and at Concord.

There were many American soldiers near Boston. But they needed a good leader. Who would this leader be? Almost all the members of Congress wanted the same man. That man was George Washington. They asked George Washington to become Commander-in-Chief of the new American army. They said that his first job would be to drive the English soldiers out of Boston. Would he take such a hard job?

George Washington was a wealthy man. He owned a large farm at Mount Vernon in Virginia. He led a very pleasant life at Mount Vernon.

18. Americans Win Their Freedom

If he became Commander-in-Chief he would have to give up that pleasant life. He would often be cold, tired, and hungry. His life would be in danger.

But Washington did not hesitate. He said that if his country needed him he would be happy to serve. He also said that he would not take any money for doing it.

In the picture above we see Washington taking command of his army. This happened at Cambridge, Massachusetts, on June 3, 1775.

Washington Captures Boston. Washington drilled his soldiers and trained them to fight. He captured the hills around Boston. General Gage, the leader of the English soldiers, decided it was not safe to stay in Boston. In March, 1776, he sailed away with his soldiers. He went to Halifax, in Nova Scotia.

George Washington and his American soldiers marched into Boston. The people cheered George Washington. They were happy to be free once more.

A War for Freedom. In July, 1776, Washington heard that Congress had adopted the Declaration of Independence. He had the Declaration of Independence read to his men.

Until this time Washington and his men had been fighting for fair treatment. Now they were fighting for a free country. Washington knew that the English would not allow the colonies to be free if they could help it. He knew that the war would be long and bitter.

The war was now being fought for freedom, or independence. That is why it is often called the War for Independence. It is also called the American Revolution.

The Americans Faced a Big Task. George Washington knew that he faced a big task. If you will look again at the picture at the beginning of this chapter you will see that his soldiers did not even have uniforms. They did not have very much of anything. They did not have enough guns or powder. They did not have enough food. They did not have enough money to buy these things.

Washington's army was small. He had no navy at all.

He was fighting England. England was the most powerful country in the world at that time. England had a large, well trained army. England had the world's largest navy.

The Americans thought they could win, but they knew it would be a long, hard war.

The Americans Had Two Things in Their Favor. How could a poor group of colonies hope to defeat a powerful England? The Americans had two things in their favor:

1. The Americans were fighting for their homes and for their freedom. They felt that these things were worth fighting for. They were worth dying for, if necessary. Men can always fight better when they know they are fighting for something important. The English, on the other hand, were fighting far from their own homes. Many of them were not very much interested in the war. They did not have as much to fight for.

2. The Americans had good leaders. The best leader of all was George Washington. Washington was a good planner. He was very brave. And he would not give up. When it seemed that the Americans were almost certain to lose, Washington kept on fighting. He cheered his men when they were cold, and tired, and hungry. His men looked up to him and followed his example. They kept on fighting after most men would have given up.

FAMOUS AMERICANS

Thomas Jefferson owned a large estate in Virginia. He could have led a very easy life. But Thomas Jefferson worked almost all his life for his country and the people.

Jefferson believed in liberty and self-government. He said the people could be trusted to do what was right. Congress asked Jefferson to write the Declaration of Independence. In the Declaration, Jefferson wrote that "all men are created equal." He also wrote that "everyone has a right to life, liberty, and the pursuit of happiness."

During the last years of the War, Jefferson was elected Governor of Virginia. One day, some English soldiers were sent to capture him, but he escaped just in time. After the War, Jefferson held many important offices. He became the third president of the United States in 1801. He was president for eight years.

One of the last things Jefferson did was to help start the University of Virginia. Jefferson always thought that schools were very important. He said that people should have a good education if they were to rule themselves. Jefferson died on July 4, 1826. This was exactly fifty years after the Declaration of Independence was signed.

Today we Americans are proud of our liberty and our self-government. Thomas Jefferson is one of the men we can thank for these blessings.

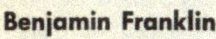

Benjamin Franklin

The Americans had a fine leader in Benjamin Franklin. Although he was born in Boston, Franklin ran away to Philadelphia at 16 and made that city his home. Ben had learned the printing trade in his brother's printing shop in Boston.

In Philadelphia Ben Franklin soon saved enough money to open his own printing shop. Then he printed the records and official papers of the Philadelphia Assembly. He also wrote a newspaper and a book of wise and witty sayings.

Benjamin Franklin served his country in many ways. He formed the first volunteer fire department and organized the first hospital in America. Franklin opened the first public library in Philadelphia because he wanted others to love books as he loved them.

CHARLES CARROLL

ONE of the 57 men who signed the Declaration of Independence was a Catholic. He was Charles Carroll of Carrollton.

Charles Carroll was born in Maryland. Because Catholic schools were not allowed in Maryland at the time, Charles was sent to school in France. He came back to Maryland when he was 27 years old. He had been away from the time he was a boy of 11.

He was elected to many important offices. Since Catholics could not vote, the people who elected Charles Carroll were Protestants. He helped write many new laws for Maryland. One of these laws allowed Catholics to build churches and schools for the first time in many years.

He was also a member of the Congress that adopted the Declaration of Independ-

Pulaski   Kosciusko

OTHERS WHO CONTRIBUTED TO AMERICAN FREEDOM

Men from many lands helped the Americans to win the war against England. Count Casimir Pulaski of Poland organized the American cavalry. Another Polish patriot, Thaddeus Kosciusko, planned the defenses at Saratoga and West Point. Washington's army at Valley Forge was drilled by a German, Baron Friedrich von Steuben. In Virginia the Frenchman, Marquis de Lafayette, helped in defeating General Cornwallis at Yorktown. This ended the war.

Von Steuben   Lafayette

of Carrollton

ence. As he signed his name to the Declaration someone told him that the English might take away all his land and all his money.

"No," said someone else, "there are several men named Charles Carroll. The English will not know which one this is."

Charles Carroll then picked up the pen. After his name he wrote the words "of Carrollton."

"They cannot mistake me now," he said with a knowing smile.

Charles Carroll lived to be 86 years old. He was still living after all the other signers of the Declaration had died. That is why he became known as "the last of the signers."

His cousin John Carroll became the first Bishop in the United States. He also became the first Archbishop in the United States. Always a good Catholic, Charles Carroll was asked before he died what had made him a happy man. "That I have practiced the duties of my religion," he said.

Washington Is Driven From New York. Washington took 11,000 soldiers to New York City. The English wished to capture this city for two reasons:
1. It had the best harbor in America.
2. If the English took this city they would be between the Southern States and the New England States.

General Howe attacked New York with 35,000 men. This was almost three times as many men as Washington had. Washington was defeated, but he saved his army. He escaped into New Jersey.

After Washington was driven from New York, he wanted to know what the English planned to do next. A young captain named Nathan Hale said he would try to find out. He went into the English camp. He pretended to be a Dutch school teacher. He found out what he wanted to know. He started back to Washington's camp. The English found out he was a spy and arrested him. In war time, spies are usually put to death. Nathan Hale was hanged. As the rope was put around his neck, he said: "I only regret that I have but one life to give for my country."

Washington Wins Two Great Battles. The English army drove Washington's army all the way across New Jersey. Many of Washington's men left the army and went back to their farms. Many died. Once he had 11,000 men; now he had only 3,000 men left. These men were dressed in rags. They did not have enough food or enough ammunition. It seemed that the Americans had lost the war. One of the English generals, Lord Cornwallis, was so sure the war was over that he sent his baggage aboard a ship. He was ready to sail back to England.

Then, on Christmas night in 1776, Washington led his men across the Delaware River. At Trenton they took an English army by surprise. It was made up of German soldiers called Hessians. These soldiers were paid to fight for the English. The Americans won a big victory.

Lord Cornwallis took his baggage off the ship. He rushed to New Jersey with a large army. Washington cut off part of Cornwallis's army and captured it at Princeton. Cornwallis hurried back to New York. He left all of New Jersey in Washington's hands.

Washington had showed the English that the war was not over.

General Burgoyne Surrenders. The English had failed to end the war quickly. They thought of a plan which they believed would finally beat the Americans. General Burgoyne was in

18. Americans Win Their Freedom

Montreal. He was to march down through New York State with a large army. When he met the English soldiers who were in New York, the colonies would be cut in two. Then it would be easy for the English to defeat the Americans.

Burgoyne ran into trouble from the start. As he marched through the forest, Americans shot at his army from behind stones and trees. The Americans cut trees and made them fall across the road. This caused Burgoyne to travel very slowly.

The Americans kept Burgoyne's men from getting food. Then they surrounded his army. He could not get any help. Burgoyne surrendered at Saratoga, New York, on October 17, 1777.

People in all the colonies were happy when they learned that General Burgoyne had surrendered. "This shows that we can defeat England's best armies," Americans said.

France had been wishing to come into the war on the side of the Americans. But first, the French wanted to be sure that they had a chance of winning the war. After Burgoyne's surrender the French knew that the Americans were good fighters. They came into the war on the American side. France was a powerful country with a big army and a big navy. She would be able to give the colonies much help. Later, Spain and Holland also declared war against England.

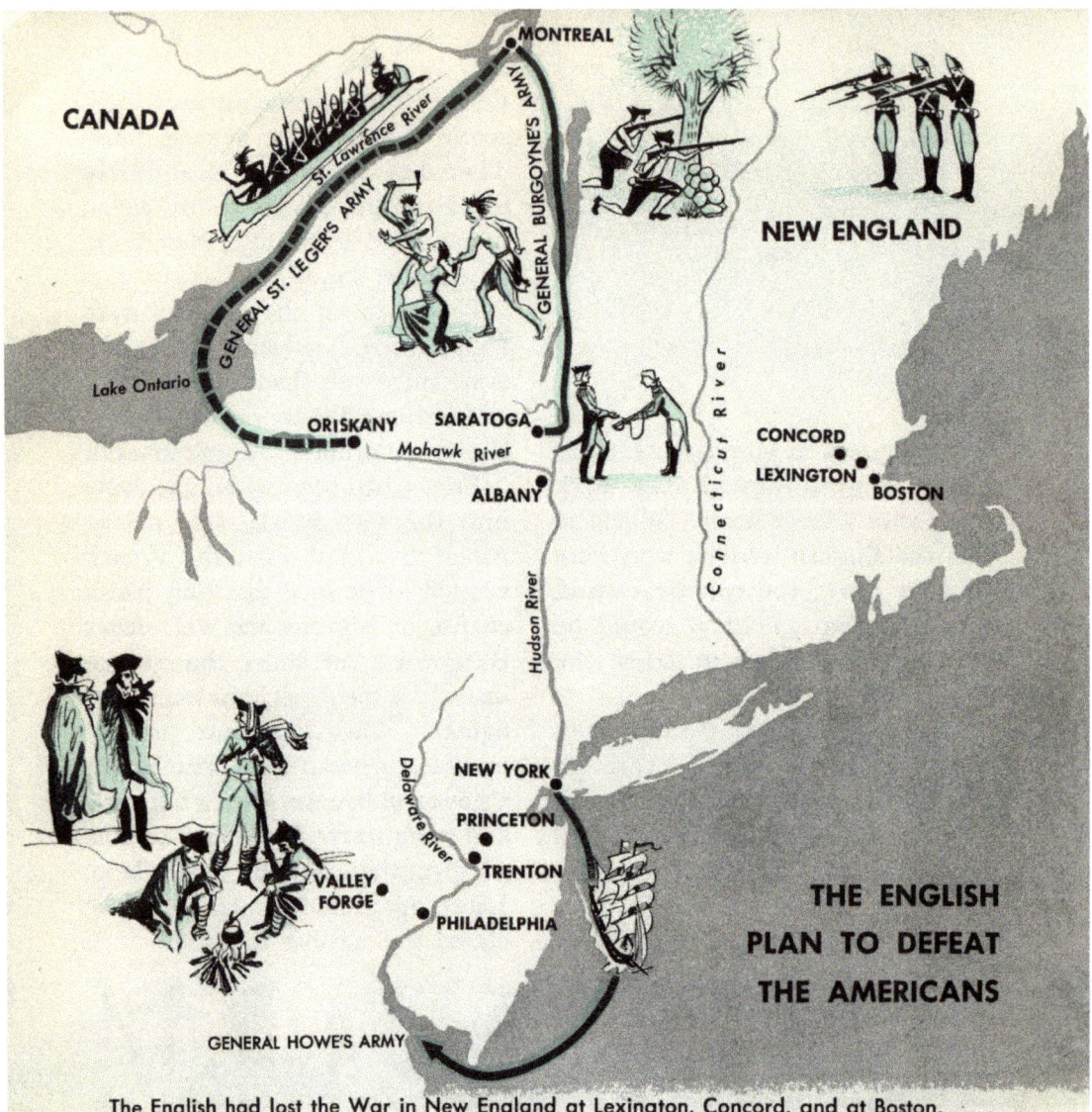

The English had lost the War in New England at Lexington, Concord, and at Boston.

Now they had a plan to win the war by separating the colonies. Three English armies were to invade New York and divide the New England Colonies from the Middle Colonies. The armies were to meet at Albany.

The first army came down from Canada but was badly beaten at Saratoga.

The second army, also from Canada, came across the State but also was defeated by the Americans at Oriskany before it reached Albany.

The third army General changed his mind and instead of going to Albany moved his army to Philadelphia. Thus ended the great English plan to defeat the Americans.

General Washington's troubles were not over. He had gained time by these victories, but he still had to drive the English from the Middle Colonies before the War would be over.

Washington Spends a Terrible Winter at Valley Forge. In the fall of 1777, General Howe led a large army from New York to Philadelphia. At that time Philadelphia was the largest city in the colonies. It was also the city in which the Continental Congress had been holding their meetings.

Washington tried to keep Howe from taking Philadelphia. But Howe defeated Washington in two battles.

After Howe's men went into Philadelphia, Washington stayed close by. His men set up winter quarters at Valley Forge, Pennsylvania.

In Philadelphia Howe's men lived in warm houses. They had plenty to eat. They went to many banquets and parties.

At Valley Forge, Washington's men lived in rude shacks. They suffered from the cold. They did not have enough to eat. Their clothes were in tatters. Many had no shoes. Their sore feet left bloodstains on the snow.

Washington suffered along with his men. He told them to keep up their courage. He prayed for help. Somehow, the little army lasted through the terrible winter.

In the spring, the English in Philadelphia learned that a big French fleet was on its way across the ocean. The English knew they could not defend the city against this fleet. They left Philadelphia and hurried back to New York.

Except for those in New York, there were no English soldiers left in the Middle Colonies.

Americans Win Battles at Sea. At the beginning of the Revolution the Americans had no navy at all. England had the largest navy in the world. The English did not think they would be in any danger from the Americans at sea. They soon found that they were mistaken.

The Americans allowed merchant ships to carry guns and sink English ships. These merchant ships were called privateers. The privateers damaged British shipping.

Later in the war, the Americans built a small navy. Captain John Barry became the first officer in this navy. Barry had been born in Ireland and he was a Catholic. He captured many ships which were carrying supplies to the English soldiers.

British warships in the Delaware River were blocking American boats and supplying the British army. Barry decided to stop this.

One night he led four small boatloads of men quietly down the river. At sunrise they were alongside a British warship. Barry's men leaped aboard the warship and quickly took over. The British were

18. Americans Win Their Freedom

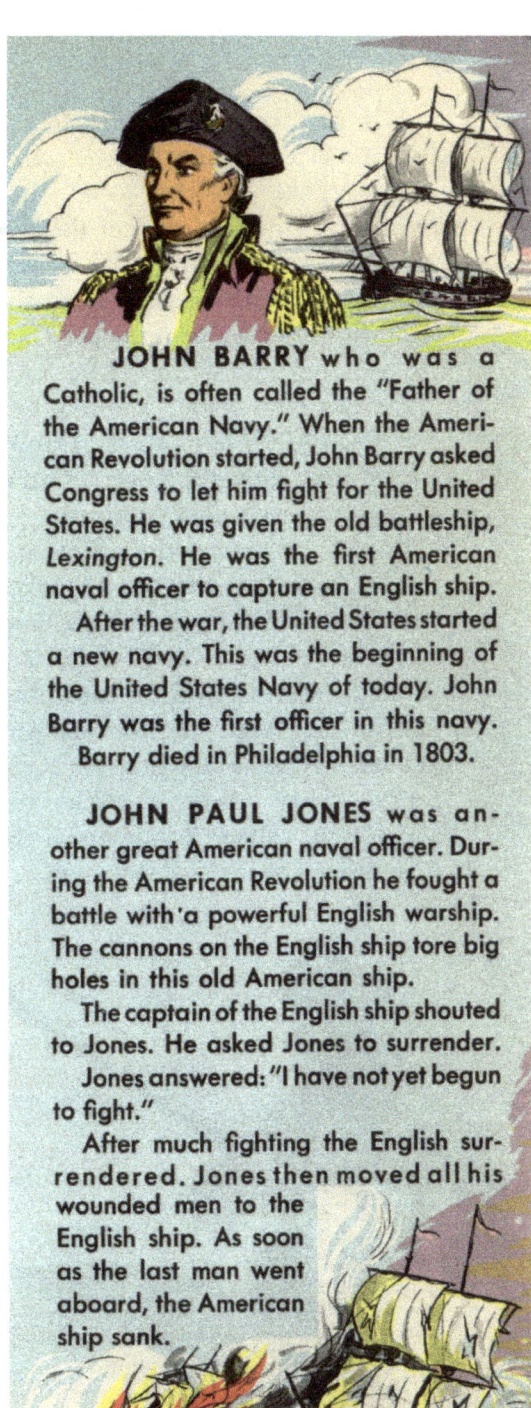

JOHN BARRY who was a Catholic, is often called the "Father of the American Navy." When the American Revolution started, John Barry asked Congress to let him fight for the United States. He was given the old battleship, *Lexington*. He was the first American naval officer to capture an English ship.

After the war, the United States started a new navy. This was the beginning of the United States Navy of today. John Barry was the first officer in this navy. Barry died in Philadelphia in 1803.

JOHN PAUL JONES was another great American naval officer. During the American Revolution he fought a battle with a powerful English warship. The cannons on the English ship tore big holes in this old American ship.

The captain of the English ship shouted to Jones. He asked Jones to surrender.

Jones answered: "I have not yet begun to fight."

After much fighting the English surrendered. Jones then moved all his wounded men to the English ship. As soon as the last man went aboard, the American ship sank.

too surprised to fight. Barry and his men also captured four supply ships near by.

Another famous officer in the American navy was John Paul Jones. Jones was such a daring seaman that he even sailed close to the coast of England. He sank many ships there.

In command of an old broken-down French boat, the *Bon Homme Richard* Jones battled with a crack new British warship, the *Serapis*. Fighting was fierce, but Jones and his men won.

Winning the West. At the time of the American Revolution when people spoke of "the west" they meant the land just west of the Appalachian Mountains. This was only a few hundred miles from the Atlantic coast. Few people had crossed the mountains. Two men made this part of our country better known. They were Daniel Boone and George Rogers Clark. These men are called pioneers.

Daniel Boone, the Pioneer. Daniel Boone's father was a Quaker who settled in Pennsylvania and then moved to North Carolina. Daniel loved to go off on exploring trips to the West. In 1773 he persuaded his family to move to Kentucky. They made a settlement which was called Boonesborough. Five other families joined them.

One day while Boone and some of his men were out searching for salt, they were captured by the Indians. The Indians brought Daniel to their camp at Detroit. The Chief liked him and adopted him into the tribe with great ceremony. Afterwards the Indians let Daniel go hunting. He never returned to the camp, but went home to warn his friends of a coming Indian attack.

The American Revolution was going on at this time. Soon the Indians who were allies of the English attacked. The Americans at Boonesborough fought them off. After the war Boone thought too many people were crowding Kentucky. He wanted more "elbow room" so he moved farther west into what has become Missouri.

The Northwest Territory. The Ohio Valley was rich country. France had lost it to the English in the French and Indian War. Now the Americans wanted it. England had made it part of Canada.

There were few settlements in this vast territory. A few forts were held by English soldiers. There were Fort Kaskaskia on the Mississippi River and Fort Vincennes near the Wabash River. If the Americans could capture these forts the whole northwestern territory would be turned over to them.

George Rogers Clark Conquers the Ohio Country. Most of the fighting in the American Revolution was done along the seacoast, but George Rogers Clark fought in the Ohio country. With a small force of men Clark captured several forts along the Ohio and Mississippi rivers.

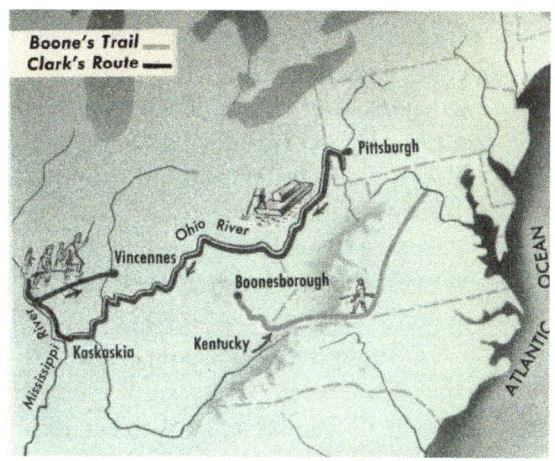

Kaskaskia was taken by surprise during a dance at the British fort on July 4, 1778. Most of the settlers in Vincennes, 200 miles away, were Catholic. Father Gibault was present at the surrender of Kaskaskia. He liked the Americans. Father Gibault went to Vincennes and told the French people that the Americans were coming to capture the fort. He told them not to resist. The French agreed. This was a great help to Clark.

The following winter George Rogers Clark and his men set out to capture Fort Vincennes. There were many English soldiers in Vincennes. Clark knew that his only chance was to take the English by surprise. He knew that the English would not be expecting an attack in the middle of winter. His men walked more than 200 miles. Often they had to walk through icy water.

Clark took the English by surprise. He captured Vincennes. All the Ohio country was now in the hands of the Americans. When the treaty of peace was signed, this vast territory was given to the United States.

This territory became known as the Northwest Territory. It is a region of beauty and of great natural wealth. Five states have been made out of this territory. They are Ohio, Indiana, Illinois, Michigan, and Wisconsin.

The War Ends. The English were badly beaten in the North, so they turned to the South.

At first the English won all the big battles in the South. But they could never destroy the American armies. "We fight, get beaten, and fight again," said one of the American generals.

The English seemed to suffer more in winning than the Americans did in losing. General Cornwallis saw that his men were very tired from all the marching and fighting. He also knew that they needed more food and more ammunition. He took his army to Yorktown on the seacoast. Here he waited for more help from England.

This was the chance that Washington had been waiting for. He asked the French fleet to go to Yorktown. He marched to Yorktown with his army. Many French soldiers went there also. Cornwallis found that he was completely surrounded. The French warships cut him off by sea. American and French soldiers cut him off by land.

There was nothing for Cornwallis to do but surrender. He did so on October 18, 1781.

18. Americans Win Their Freedom

"It's all over," said a leader of the British government when he heard the news.

King George III still hoped that the United States could be conquered. But the English had had enough. Their best armies in the United States had surrendered. Their ships had been sunk in every part of the world. They wanted no more fighting.

England Accepts the United States As a Free Nation. Fighting ended when Cornwallis surrendered in October, 1781. The peace treaty was not signed until almost two years later, in September, 1783.

In the peace treaty England agreed that the Americans were "a free and independent nation." This new country extended from the Atlantic Ocean to the Mississippi.

England gave Florida and the land along the Gulf of Mexico to Spain. Spain had also fought against England.

The map shows the boundaries of our country after the signing of the peace treaty in 1783.

Washington Leaves the Army. It was June 5, 1775, when George Washington took command of the American army. It was December 23, 1783, when he left the army. He had been Commander-in-Chief for more than eight years.

Washington was sad when he said goodbye to his men. He was sorry to leave the men who had worked with him for so many years. But he was glad that the war was over. And he was glad that he could go back to live in peace at Mount Vernon.

He did not know that his country would call upon him once more. He did not know about the great task still to come.

But his first great task had been done well. He had led the Americans in a great war. That war had made Americans a free nation.

STUDY LESSON

WHO AM I? Write the name of each person listed. Next to it write the sentence which tells you about the person.

1. Nathan Hale
2. John Barry
3. George Rogers Clark
4. General Howe
5. Lord Cornwallis
6. John Paul Jones
7. General Burgoyne

a. I surrendered my army at Yorktown.
b. I am a famous American navy officer who sank many British ships.
c. I was hanged by the British as a spy.
d. With my men I captured forts along the Ohio and Mississippi rivers.
e. I surrendered to the American army at Saratoga.
f. With my army I drove George Washington out of New York.
g. I was the first officer of the American navy.

18. Americans Win Their Freedom

WHAT AM I? Write each place name and after it the phrase that explains it.

1. Valley Forge
2. Yorktown
3. Trenton
4. Saratoga
5. Vincennes
6. Philadelphia

a. largest city of the colonies at the time of the Revolutionary War.
b. fort captured by Clark in the Ohio country.
c. Washington's winter quarters.
d. city where Washington surprised the British army on Christmas night.
e. place where Burgoyne surrendered.
f. place where Cornwallis surrendered.

SOMETHING TO THINK ABOUT. Think carefully before you answer these questions.

1. Why do you think Washington wanted to serve his country?
2. Why did the American soldiers have more to fight for than the English?
3. Do you think that spies are needed in war time?
4. What kept Washington's army at Valley Forge ready to fight despite much suffering and hardship?
5. Why do you think France helped the Americans during the Revolutionary War?
6. Why did the English feel they would have no trouble defeating the colonies?
7. Why did the English want to capture New York City?
8. Why was Cornwallis and his army not able to leave Yorktown by sea?

DATES TO REMEMBER. Write each date in column A. Next to it write the phrase in column B, that matches the date.

A	B
1. 1781	a. Washington crossed the Delaware.
2. 1783	b. Burgoyne's surrender.
3. 1777	c. Cornwallis surrendered at Yorktown.
4. 1776	d. Treaty of Peace signed.

WORDS TO KNOW. Write a sentence using each of these words. Look them up in your dictionary if you are not sure of the meaning.

congress   privateers   territory   fleet

WHERE IS IT? Answer each question in a complete sentence.

1. To what state would we go to visit Mount Vernon?
2. What river did Washington's army have to cross to reach the city of Trenton?
3. What states were made out of the Ohio country after the Revolutionary War?
4. What were the eastern and western boundaries of the new nation after the Revolution?

How Our Nation Began

GAMES . . ART . .

SCRAPBOOK OF FAMOUS PEOPLE

ADD THESE STORIES, WITH PICTURES IF POSSIBLE, TO YOUR SCRAPBOOK.

IF YOU WERE A WEALTHY FARMER IN 1775, WOULD YOU HAVE LEFT YOUR PLANTATION TO LEAD THE HARD LIFE OF A SOLDIER FOR EIGHT YEARS? WOULD YOU OFFER TO SERVE IN THE ARMY FOR NO PAY? GEORGE WASHINGTON DID. WRITE A STORY ABOUT GEORGE WASHINGTON.

WHAT DID NATHAN HALE SAY WHEN THE BRITISH WERE ABOUT TO HANG HIM FOR HELPING WASHINGTON? IN A FEW SENTENCES, TELL ABOUT THAT BRAVE, LOYAL AMERICAN.

THIS IS HOW IT HAPPENED

READ HENRY WADSWORTH LONGFELLOW'S POEM "THE MIDNIGHT RIDE OF PAUL REVERE" AND MAKE A PLAY FROM THE POEM.

NAME GAME

USING PERSONS WHO HAVE APPEARED IN UNIT FOUR, PLAY THE GAME WHICH WAS DESCRIBED AT THE END OF UNIT ONE.

18. Americans Win Their Freedom

BOOKS...PLAYS

SEEING OUR CONTINENT

DRAW OR TRACE A MAP OF NORTH AMERICA. THIS MAP SHOULD SHOW NORTH AMERICA AFTER THE TREATY OF PARIS OF 1763. COLOR ENGLISH LAND RED, SPANISH LAND YELLOW, AND FRENCH LAND BLUE. THEN DRAW ANOTHER MAP REPRESENTING NORTH AMERICA AFTER THE TREATY OF PARIS OF 1783. COLOR THE SAME WAY BUT MAKE THE NEW NATION GREEN.

IT'S FUN TO DRAW

HERE IS A CHANCE TO USE YOUR IMAGINATION. CAN YOU IMAGINE WHAT GOOD TARGETS THE BRITISH RED COATS MADE FOR THE MINUTE MEN AND AMERICAN SHARPSHOOTERS? DRAW A PICTURE OF THE MINUTE MEN STANDING IN A LINE ACROSS THE ROAD TO CONCORD WITH THE COLUMN OF BRITISH TROOPS COMING STRAIGHT AT THEM. MOST OF THE BRITISH DIED WHILE THEY WERE RETREATING TO BOSTON. DRAW A PICTURE OF THIS RETREAT. CAN YOU IMAGINE THE SURPRISE OF THE ENEMY WHEN WASHINGTON ATTACKED TRENTON ON CHRISTMAS NIGHT? DRAW A PICTURE OF WASHINGTON CROSSING THE DELAWARE RIVER WITH HIS TROOPS. CAN YOU IMAGINE WHAT IT MUST HAVE BEEN LIKE AT VALLEY FORGE? DRAW A PICTURE OF OUR SOLDIERS IN CAMP.

INFORMATION CENTER

THESE BOOKS WILL TELL YOU MORE ABOUT THE PEOPLE AND EVENTS IN THIS UNIT.

AULAIRE	BEN FRANKLIN	DOUBLEDAY
	GEORGE WASHINGTON	DOUBLEDAY
EDMONDS	MATCHLOCK GUN	DODD
LAWSON	WATCHWORDS OF LIBERTY	LITTLE
PACE	EARLY AMERICAN: THE STORY OF PAUL REVERE	SCRIBNER
WILLS AND SAUNDERS	BEN AND ME	LITTLE
	THOSE WHO DARED	LITTLE

Index and Glossary

A

adventure – A trip to unknown places with excitement and danger; 22, 25
Africa, 32-33, 35, 136
  Diaz reaches the tip of, 36
  Da Gama rounds, 46
  New England trade with, 136
Albany, NY, 92, 95
Albemarle, 126
Algonquins, 78, 79. See also American Indians.
America, naming of, 49
American Indians, 5-6, 43, 44, 45, 69, 70
  discover America, 12
  gifts of, 13
  in French and Indian War, 149-14
  148-149
  in Mexico, 58-61
  in Plymouth, 106
  in South America, 63
  in the Southwest, 11
  in Virginia, 69, 70, 71
  naming of, 43
  Penn and, 120
  Plains, 10-11
  Spain's treatment of, 64-65
  See also under tribe names. American Revolution, 168-184
  See also revolution.
ammunition – Bullets, shells, grenades, and bombs which are thrown against the enemy in war.
Ark, the, 124
  assemblies, colonial, 74, 118, 137, 156-157
assembly – A gathering of people, as for law making; a congress or law-making body.
  the first, in America, 74
Auriesville, NY, 80
Aztecs, 58-59

B

Bahamas, 43
Balboa, discovers Pacific Ocean, 50
Baltimore, Lord, 125, 126
Barry, Capt., 178-179
Berkeley, Lord, 118
Black Robes, 80, 82-85
Blessed Virgin appears, 60-61
boats, Northmen's, 14-15
Bon Homme Richard, 179
book making, 20, 34, picture story
Boone, Daniel, 180
Boonesborough, KY, 180
Boston, MA, 159, 160-161, 163
  settlement of, 107
  Tea Party, 160-161
  See also Massacre, Boston.
Braddock, Gen., 149- 150
Bradford, Gov. William, 103, 104, 105
braves, Indian soldiers, 8, 125
Bunker Hill, Battle of, 164
Burgoyne, Gen. John, 174-175

C

Cabot, John, 48-49, 68, 146
California, 65
Calvert, Leonard, 125
canonize – To call a person a saint.
Cape of Good Hope, 36
Cape Verde, 35
Carolinas, the, 126
Carroll, Archbishop John, 172-173
Carroll, Charles, 172-173
Carteret, George, 118
Gov. Philip, 118
Cartier, 77
Carver, Gov. John, 105
Catholic Church,
  and the American Indians, 9, 59-61, 64-65, 80-85

Cortez and, 59
in England, 102
in Greenland, 17
Our Lady of Guadalupe, 60, 61, 65
in Maryland, 124-126
in New Jersey, 118
in Pennsylvania, 120, 131
Prince Henry and the, 35
Spanish settlers and, 64-65, 66
See also Catholics in our early
history, *and* Catholic religion
Catholic religion
as France's gift, 80-85
and the Northmen, 16, 17
as Spain's gift, 64-65, 66
Catholics in our history,
in the American Revolution, 172-173, 181
in Maryland, 124-126
in Pennsylvania, 120
See also under names of, e.g.
Father Marquette, Archbishop
and Charles Carroll, Kateri
Tekakwitha, Father Farmer,
Dongan, Prince Henry, etc.
Champlain, founds Quebec, 78-79
Charleston, 126
Chesapeake Bay, 69
Church of England, 102, 103, 140
Clark, George Rogers, 180, 181-182
colonists – People who live in a colony or take
part in founding a colony.
See also settlers,
declare freedom, 156-166
effect of French and Indian War on, 153
explained, 146
colony – 1. A group of people who move from
their native land to settle elsewhere but
remain subjects of the mother country.
2. The place settled by any such group.
explained, 70
Columbus, 6, 26, 37, 38-45

discovers America, 38-45
importance of, 44, 46
Concord, Battle of, 162-163
congress – A meeting or assembly,
especially of people elected to
make laws.
Congress,
    First Continental, 162
    Second Continental, 164-165
Connecticut, 110
constitution – The basic rules governing
a nation or state,
first written, 110
Cornwallis, Lord, 174
    surrender of, 182
Coronado, searches for "Seven Cities," 64
Cortez, conquers Aztecs, 58-59
cotton, 138, 140
Crusades, 20-26

D

da Gama, reaches Far East first, 46
Dare, Virginia, 126
declaration – The act of declaring or
making something known. The paper
containing the declaration.
Declaration of Independence – The
paper which said that the English colonies
were free of England; 164-165, 170
Delaware,
and Penn, 121
Swedes and Dutch settle, 94
Diego, 60-61
De Soto, discovers the Mississippi; 63, 83
Diaz, rounds Africa's tip, 36
discovery of America
by Europeans, 42-43
by Indians, 12
Dongan, Gov. Thomas, 117, feature story
Dove, the 124
Duquesne, Fort, 149-150

Dutch in New York, 90-92, 95, 114-116
Dutch, Pennsylvania, 120

E

Elizabeth, NJ, beginning of, 118
Ericson, Leif, 15-18, 44
    finds North America, 17
Eric the Red, 15
explorers – People who go through or travel in a place or region in order to find out more about it.
  Dutch. *See* Hudson.
  English. *See* Cabot.
  French. *See* Cartier, Champlain, La Salle, *and* Father Marquette;
  Italian. *See* Cabot, Columbus, Marco Polo, Vespucci, *and* Verrazano.
  Portuguese. *See* Diaz, da Gama, *and* Prince Henry's sailors.
  Spanish. *See* Columbus, Coronado, Magellan, Pizarro, *and* Ponce de Leon.

F

Far East – The countries of eastern Asia, 23, 28-30, 32, 35, 46, 51, 52, 90, 91
  Da Gama reaches, 46
  Magellan reaches, 51
  Marco Polo in, 28-31
  Prince Henry's interest in, 35
Farmer, Father, 118
farmers, colonial, 130-131, 132-133, 134, 140.
    See also Southern planters
First Continental Congress, 162
fishermen
  French in New World, 76
  New England, 136
fleet – A group of warships that are all under the same commander.
Florida, 64
Fort
  Amsterdam, 115
  Christina, 94, 95
  Duquesne, 149, 150
  Kaskaskia, 180, 181
  Orange, 92, 95
  Pitt, 150
  Vincennes, 180, 181-182
France in the American Revolution, 175, 182
Franciscan missions, 65
Franklin, Ben, 162
freedom – State of being free or at liberty; independence.
  of religion. Permission to practice one's own religion,
    in Maryland, 124-126
    in New Jersey, 118
    in Pennsylvania, 119, 131
    in Providence, 109
    none in England, 102-103
    none in New England, 108
    none in the South, 140
French and Indian War, 146-153
  effects of the, 153
Fundamental Orders of Connecticut, 110
fur trade,
  French, 78, 79, 84
  in New York, 93, 115, 126, 130
  picture story, 92-93

G

Gage, Gen. Thomas, 161, 163, 164, 168, 169
Genoa, Italy, 25, 30, 48
  merchants of, 25, 38
George III, King, 158-161, 183
Georgia, 127-128
German settlers, 120-121
Germantown, PA, 120-121
Gibault, Father, 181
government – Control of a nation or state,
  of English colonies, 137, 156-157
    See also assemblies, *and* constitution

Great Khan, 28-30
Great Lakes, 79, 82, 88
Greenland
   Northmen in, 15, 16, 17
Gutenberg, John
   picture story, 34

H

Hale Nathan, 173
Half Moon, the, 90
Hartford, CT, founding of, 110
Henry, Patrick, 162
Henry of Portugal, Prince, 32-35, 36
Holy Wars, 20-26
homes, colonial, 115-116, 134, 139. *See also* houses
Hooker, Thomas,
   founds Connecticut, 110
hospitality, Southern, explained, 139
houses, Dutch, 115-116
   colonial, 130-131
   New England, 134-135
   Southern, 139
   Swedish, 94
Howe, General, 173, 177
Hudson, Henry,
   discovers Hudson River, 90-91
Hurons (hu'rdnz), 78, 80

I

Iceland (Is'ldnd),
   discovery by Northmen, 15
Incas, the
   Pizarro conquers, 63
independence
   State of being free, or under no one else's rule or control; freedom; self-government.
Declaration of Independence, 164-165, 170
Indians, American 5-6, 43, 44, 45, 69, 70, 71, 90, 91, 92
   Algonquin, 78, 79
   Aztec, 58-59
   Blessed Mother and, 60-61
   Huron, 78, 80
   Inca, 63
   Iroquois, 78, 80, 149
   See also under given names, e.g., Massassoit, Juan Diego, etc.
Iroquois, the, 78, 80, 149

J

James I, King of England, 69
Jamestown VA,
   founding of, 68-72, 124
Jefferson, Thomas, 165
Jerusalem, Isr.,
   taken by Crusaders, 24
Jesuit martyrs, 80
Jogues, Father Isaac, 80
Jones, John Paul, 179
John, King of Portugal, 36
Joliet, 83-84

K

Kaskaskia
   taking of Fort, 180, 181
Kateri Tekakwitha, 81
Khan Great, 28-30
kitchen, colonial
   Dutch, 116
   New England, 135
   Pennsylvania, 130-131

L

La Salle, 86-87, 146
law. A rule which a nation or smaller group of people agrees to follow.
Lexington, MA, Battle of, 162-163
life
   Crusades change, 26
   in 11th century Europe, 20

in English colonies, 130-140
in Middle colonies, 115-116, 130-133
in the Near East, 23
in New England, 134-136
in New Netherland, 115-116
in Southern colonies, 138-140
Los Angeles, 64

M

Magellan, 50-52
Manhattan Island, 90, 92, 115
maps,
  Africa, Diaz rounds, 36
  Cabot's voyage, 48
  Cartier's voyage, 77
  Champlain's voyages, 79
  Columbus, 1st voyage of, 45
  Crusades, 21 Diaz, 36
  Dutch in New York, 91
  English possessions, 96
  French possessions, 88, 96
  Indians of North America, 10, 12
  Magellan circles the world, 52
  Marquette's explorations, 85
  Maryland, 125
  Middle Colonies, 122
  New England, 108, 112
  North America after 1763, 152
  North America after 1783, 183
  Northmen's voyages, 14
  Ohio country, 147, 181
  Portugal in the New World, 62
  Southern colonies, 128
  Spain in the New World, 62, 96
  trade routes, Old World, 29
  United States of America, 183
  Verrazano, voyage of, 77
  Virginia and Maryland, 125
  voyages, 14, 45, 48, 77, 85
Marco Polo, 32
  and his travels, 28-30
  Book of, 30-31, 39
Marquette, Father, 82-85
  explores Mississippi, 83-84
martyrs, Persons who die rather than give up their religion.
  French, 80, 81
  Indian girl, 81
  Spanish, 64-65
Maryland, Catholic
  colony of, 124-126
Massachusetts Bay Colony, 104, 107-108
  Bay Company, 107
massacre. The cruel killing of a number of persons.
  Boston Massacre, 159
Massassoit, Chief, 106, 109
Mayflower, the, 104
  Mayflower Compact, the, 105
merchants. Persons who carry on trade; storekeepers; 25, 28, 38
merchant ships. The trading ships of a nation;
  in the American Revolution, 178
Mexico, history of, 58-62
  Our Lady of Guadalupe, 60-61
Middle Colonies, 114-122
  Dutch in the, 90-93, 95, 96, 115
  life in the, 115-116, 130-133
  Swedes in the, 94-96
Minuit, Peter,
  buys Manhattan, 92
  in New Sweden, 94
Minute Men, 162-163, 164
missionaries, 6. *See under* their own names e.g., Father Marquette, Father Jogues, etc.
missions. Places where missionaries work.
  Spanish, 65
Mississippi River, 146, 153
  discovered by de Soto, 63, 83
  explored by Marquette, 83-85
  mouth reached by LaSalle, 86-87
monastery, The buildings where monks live.

Montcalm, Gen., 151
Montezuma, 58-59
Montreal, 77
Moors. Arabs of the Moslem religion who invaded Spain until 1492.
  Spain's war with the, 40
Mount Vernon, 168
movable type, 34, picture

N

Near East, 21, 23-24
Negro slaves, 136, 139
  first in Virginia, 73
New Amsterdam, 92, 95, 114, 115
Newark, NJ, 118
New England,
  Northmen visit, 17
  Pilgrims and Puritans in, 102-112
Newfoundland,
  French in, 76
New France, 76-88
  loss of, 146-154
New Hampshire,
  settling of, 111
New Jersey,
  Colony of, 118
  in the Revolution, 173, 174
New Netherland, 92, 95, 114-116
  becomes New York, 114-115
New Orleans, founding of, 87
New Sweden, 94, 121
New World, the. The Western Hemisphere, including North America and South America;
  discovered by Europeans, 42-43
  discovered by the "Indians," 12
New York, 90-94, 114-117
  bought from the Indians, 92
noblemen, People born in high society and friends of the king.
North America
  discovered, 12, 16-17, 42-43, 48
  "Indians" in, 8-13
  Northmen in, 14-18
North American martyrs, 80-81
North Carolina, 126
Northmen, People who lived in northern Europe about a thousand years ago.
  discover America, 14-18, 44-45
Northwest Territory, the, 180-182

O

Oglethorpe, James, founds Georgia, 127
Ohio River Valley, 146, 147, 148, 149
Olaf of Norway, King, 16
Our Lord, 21, 22, 24

P

Pacific Ocean, discovered, 50
  Magellan and, 51-52
Panama, Balboa crosses, 50
papoose, A baby of North American Indians, 8
Parliament. The assembly which makes the laws of England; 156, 157, 158, 159, 160, 161, 165
  Passaic River, 118
patroons, Owners of large farms along the Hudson River when the Dutch governed New York; 92
Penn, William, 118, 119-121
Pennsylvania, colony of, 119-121
  "Dutch," 120
life in, 130-133
persecution. Injury for religious reasons; 102-103, 108, 119
Peru, history of, 63
Philadelphia, PA, laid out, 120, 121
Philippines, the, 51
picture stories,
American Revolution at sea, 179
Archbishop Carroll, 172-173
astrolabe, the, 34

Barry, Captain John, 179
   Catholic Church in English colonies, 172-173
   colonial life, 66, 111, 132-133, 154
   English colonial life, 111, 132-133
   Europeans in Revolution, 172
   Far East, wonders of the, 30
   Ferdinand, Spanish colonist, 66
   Franklin, Ben, 171
   French colonial life, 154
   fur trade in New York, 92-93
   Gutenberg, John, 34
   Indian gifts, American, 12
   Jean, a French colonist, 154
   Jefferson, Thomas, 171
   Jones, John Paul, 179
   John, a Minute Man, 166
   Kateri Tekakwitha, 81
   life in the English colonies, 111, 132-133, 154
   life in a French colony, 154
   life in a Spanish colony, 66
   Minute Man, John the, 166
   Paul, an English colonist, 111
   sailors, 34, 179
   Spanish colonial life, 66
Pilgrims, the, 102-107
pioneer, An explorer; early settler, or colonist.
   Daniel Boone as a, 180
Pitt, William, 150
Pius XII, Pope, 61
Pizarro, conquers Peru, 63
plantations, Large estates farmed by laborers.
   life on Southern, 138-140
planters, Southern, 126, 138-140
Plymouth Colony,
   Pilgrims found, 105-107
Pocahontas, 70, 71
Polo, Marco, 28-31, 43
Ponce de Leon, discovers Florida, 64
portage, explained, 84
Powhatan, Chief, 70
Prince Henry of Portugal, 32-35, 36

Princeton, NJ, battle at, 174
printing, 20, 34, 39
   press. A machine which prints from type, wood blocks, plates; etc., picture story, 34
privateers. Armed private ships with permission from the government to make war on ships of the enemy, in American Revolution, 178
Providence, RI, founding of, 109
Protestants, 102, 103
pueblo. One of the Indian villages in Arizona or New Mexico. The houses were built of stone or adobe and often had several stories; 64
Puritans, the, in Massachusetts, 107-108
Puritan Church, 135, 137

Q

Quakers, 119
Quebec,
   Battle of, 150-151
   settlement of, 78

R

Raleigh, Sir Walter, 126
religion, freedom of. *See* freedom of religion.
Revere, Paul, 163
revolution. A great change in government, especially one brought about by war, e.g., the American Revolution.
Revolution, American, 168-184
   at sea, 178-179
   causes of, 156-165
   end of, 182-183
Rhode Island, Rogers Williams founds, 109
Rolfe, John, 71

S

sailors, Seamen; 18
   new helps for, picture story, 34
   Northmen as, 14-15, 16, 18

Index and Glossary

Prince Henry's, 32-37
St. Augustine, FL, 64
St. Francis Xavier, 46
Saint Ignace Mission, 82, 85
St. Lawrence, discovery of, 77, 79
St. Malo fishermen, 76, 77
Salem
   Puritans come to, 107
Samoset, 106
San Salvador, 43
Santa Maria, the, 41, 42
Schneider, Father, 118
school for sailors, 32-33
schools, Southern, 140
Second Continental Congress, 164-165
self-government, 137, 156-157.
   See *also* assemblies, *and* government, *and* Parliament.
Serapis, the, 179
Serra, Father, 65
settlement. A colony or small village.
settlers. Colonists.
   Dutch, 90-94, 114-116, 120
   English, 68-74, 102-112, 118-120, 122, 124-129
   French, 76-88
   German, 120-121
   Swedish, 94, 95, 121
shipbuilders, New England, 136
slave. A person who is owned by another person and can be sold like a horse or cow.
slavery, Negro, 73, 136, 139
Smith, Capt. James, 69-71, 105
Snorri, first American-born white child, 17
South Carolina, settlement of, 126
Southern Colonies, 68-74, 124-129
Spain's gifts to New World, 64-65, 66
Spanish settlements, 58-66
   in California, 65
   in Mexico, 58-62
   in Peru, 63
   in the Southwest, 64-65
   in the United States, 63-65
spice. Part of a plant, used to season food; 24, 25
Squanto, 106
squaws. American Indian women; 8, 125
Stamp Act, the, 156-158
   Congress, 158
Stuvvesant, Gov. Peter, 114-115
surrender. Giving up; at Yorktown, 182
Swedes, settle Delaware, 94, 95, 121

T

tax. Money to pay for running the government, trouble over, 156-160
Texas, discovered, 87
Tekakwitha, Kateri. See Kateri Tekakwitha
tepees. The cone-shaped tents of skins, etc., used by some American Indians; 11
territory. A region controlled by another country.
tobacco, in the South, 72, 126, 138
toleration. The practice of letting everyone go to his own church.
Toleration Act, 126
tomahawk. A light ax used by Indians; 9
trade, 23, 24, 25, 26, 30-31, 138
trading post. A clearing in the forest where the Indians traded furs and where the white trappers could buy supplies
treaty. A written agreement between nations.
Treaty of Paris, the,
   after American Revolution, 185
   French and Indian War, 151
tribe. Some families who are related and a chief; 9
tutors. Private teachers; 140
type, movable, 34 picture story

U

united. Joined together so as to make one.

United States,
  birth of, 165
  Spaniards in, 63-65

V

Valley Forge, PA,
Washington at, 177
Venice, merchants of, 25, 28
Verrazano, explores North America, 76
Vespucci, Amerigo, 85, map
  writes about America, 49
Victoria, the, 51
village life in New England, 134
Vincennes, Fort, 180, 181-182
Vinland, Northmen visit, 17-18
Virginia, 68-74
voting, colonial, 137

W

Wabash River, 180
wampum. Beads made of shells used by American Indians for money; 9
Washington, George, 128, 162, 168
  and the army of the Revolution, 169, 170, 173, 174
  Commander-in-Chief, 168-169, 170
  in the French and Indian War, 146, 147, 148, 149, 150
Western Hemisphere. The half of the globe west of the Prime Meridian. Where the New World is.
White, Father Andrew, 124, 125
wigwams, 11
wilderness. A wild region with no people; 8-9
Williams, Roger, 109, 125
Wilmington, DE, founding of, 94
Wineland, 17-18
Winthrop, Gov., 107
Wolfe, Gen. 150-151

Y

Yorktown, VA,
  British surrender at, 182

www.ingramcontent.com/pod-product-compliance
Lightning Source LLC
Chambersburg PA
CBHW060923170426
43192CB00021B/2852